LIGHTHOUSES
of
New Jersey Delaware

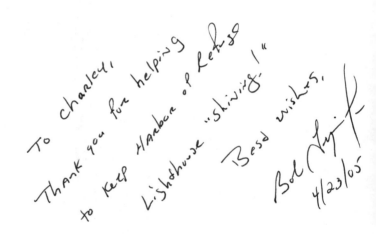

To charley,
Thank you for helping
to keep Harbor of Refuge
Lighthouse "shining!"
Best wishes,
Bob Trapani
4/23/05

HISTORY, MYSTERY, LEGENDS & LORE

Bob Trapani, Jr.

Lighthouses of New Jersey and Delaware
History, Mystery, Legends and Lore
First Edition

ISBN   1-890690-15-5

Published by
Myst and Lace Publishers, Inc.
1386 Fair Hill Lane
Elkton, Maryland 21921

Printed in the U.S.A.
in Baltimore, Maryland
by Victor Graphics

Cover Photographs by
Ann-Marie and Bob Trapani, Jr.

Typography, Layout and Cover Design
by Kathleen Okonowicz

Dedication

*This book is dedicated to Harry Spencer and Stephen Jones—
guys who lived the lighthouse life and whose friendship shines
as bright as the lights themselves.*
—Bob Trapani, Jr.

*Harry Spencer, Jr. (left) and Stephen Jones, inside Harbor of
Refuge Lighthouse, June 27, 2004*

Photo by Bob Trapani, Jr.

Acknowledgements

I would like to express special thanks to my wife, Ann-Marie
Trapani, for helping with countless hours of research, scanning and
proofreading...she is my best friend and the true light of my life.

Books are team efforts that reveal the many contributions of
others—both big and small, but all sincerely appreciated. The book you
are holding in your hand is no different. I would like to thank the
following people for their assistance:

U.S. Coast Guard Chief Michael Baroco, Hazel Brittingham,
Barbara Burgoon, James Claflin, Penny Czerwinski, Jeremy D'Entremont,
Karen DeRosa of Tuckerton Seaport, Marianna Dyal, Elinor De Wire,
U.S. Coast Guard Master Chief Dennis Dever, Tim Harrison, Stephen
Jones, Dorothy Lynch-Morris, Betty Mugnier, Steve Murray, Ed and
Kathleen Okonowicz, Scott Price, John Sarro, Harry Spencer, Jr., Ted
Stegura, U.S. Coast Guard Aids to Navigation Teams, Cape May, New
Jersey, and Philadelphia, Pennsylvania, U.S. Coast Guard Historian's
Office, and last but hardly least, the Good Lord—author of life itself.

Other books by Bob Trapani, Jr.

Journey Along the Sands:
History of the Indian River Life-Saving Station
Donning Publishing Company, Virginia Beach, Va. 2002

Guardians of the Coast: History of Delaware's Lighthouses
History Press, Charleston, S.C. (to be released in 2005)

Table of Contents

Introduction

"The lighthouse work has probably as much of romance and heroism and general interest connected with it as any government activity, and its heroism and history are of peace and protection, and it is full of interesting application of science and engineering to the helpful service of men, to the protection of life and property upon the sea. The lightkeeper stands his vigils for all humanity, asking no questions as to the nationality or purpose of him whom he directs to safety."

—George Putnam,
United States Lighthouse Commissioner, 1910-1935

In the days before roads and rail, America's waterways were its highways. Though the nation's coastal waters, bays and rivers seemed like wide open spaces of sparkling blue, the reality was that such waters were fraught with deadly dangers lurking just beneath their concealing surfaces. The treacherous hazards associated with sandy shoals or rocky ledges only grew more precarious for mariners the closer to land they sailed.

In an effort to preserve valuable ships and cargo—as well as protect the lives of the sailors of the sea—lighthouses of every shape, size and construction were established along the most dangerous locations of America's waterways.

Since the first lighthouse was constructed in colonial times—the Boston Light Station in 1716—the guiding beams of light and bellowing warnings from fog signals at light stations across the country have saved countless lives and property. In the process, the service of these stalwart sentinels has created a permanent and glorious spot within America's rich maritime heritage.

1

Little Known and Nearly Forgotten Stories

Stories of unsurpassed heroism, horrific storms and dreaded isolation abound in the history books honoring America's lighthouses, but many of the strange, mysterious, humorous and downright frightening accounts of everyday life at a light station have been lost forever in the pages of time. What irreplaceable tidbits that have survived from a bygone era shed a bright light on many human interest aspects of lighthouse life—both good times and bad.

The book you are holding is an effort to preserve a few of these glimpses into the past of real people who tended to the lights through calm and storm, loneliness and contentment . . . and their hopes and fears. The lighthouse, its keeper and the mariner they served were inseparable, and they remain so in these fascinating stories of shipwreck, humor, death and vanished lights. Such accounts also lend a hand to saving America's lighthouses from being lost forever.

Why Save Lighthouses?

The lightkeepers of the legendary United States Lighthouse Service are now all gone, as are too many of the lights they so faithfully tended to during the America's golden age of lighthouses. The fact is as we press forward in the 21st century; we can be assured that society will not build such humanitarian and inspiring edifices again. For in the age of digital technology, the need for lighthouses is deemed "obsolete."

Yet year after year, people of all ages and backgrounds are attracted to these stately sentinels that grace our coastlines and favorite vacation spots.

Many search their presence out with fervor—relishing in the romance, strength, spiritual connotation and lore that each lighthouse represents, to them personally and to the community in which it stands. But since automation removed the presence of the keepers, many of America's lighthouses stand empty and deteriorating . . . slowly "dying" with the passing of each year. Mother Nature, vandalism, erosion and, sadly, even human indifference continues to threaten countless lighthouses.

Thanks to the dedicated efforts and unwavering passion of non-profit organizations and governmental agencies, many of our nation's lighthouses have been saved from the brink of oblivion.

But, unfortunately, many more have no such reprieve from a future date with destiny.

The lighthouse preservation movement is alive and strong in America, but the effort needs more people who care to make a difference in saving a vital part of our country's heritage—a rich history that parallels the strength and prosperity of America since its inception.

Too much of our nation's lighthouse heritage has been lost already. We can ill afford to allow more of this irreplaceable history to vanish. For each time we hear of the loss of another lighthouse, a part of America dies with it.

The lighthouse is both a symbol of our proud past and a guiding beacon to a hopeful future. This fact alone should inspire us to act now to save such treasures, for once lost, their presence will not pass this way again.

Keep the Lights Shining!

Bob Trapani, Jr.
In historic Lewes, Delaware
A Gateway to Delaware Bay's Maritime Heritage
Spring 2005

Photo by Bob Trapani, Jr.

Sandy Hook Lighthouse
New Jersey

Bob Trapani, Jr.

Double Identity of Guidance and Death

The oldest existing lighthouse in America once held a haunting secret that would have made its keepers quite apprehensive about scaling the 85-foot tower in the middle of the night had they known about the fate of one unfortunate patriot. The saying, "what you don't know won't hurt you," certainly applied to the lightkeepers of Sandy Hook for over 100 years as they tended to the flame atop the historic beacon.

It all started when New York colonists created a lottery to pay for the construction of Sandy Hook Lighthouse in 1764. Ironically, though the lighthouse was financed by New Yorkers, it would stand sentinel on New Jersey soil where it could best mark the entrance to New York Harbor.

Prize of War

The massive octagonal tower was built to last, possessing a sturdy combination of a rubblestone exterior and lined brick walls on the interior. The base of the lighthouse was 39 feet in diameter and 7-feet thick—girth that would both help protect the structure from the wrath of cannon fire during the Revolutionary War while serving as a tomb for death and despair. With New York Harbor proving such a strategic military prize throughout America's fight for independence, it should come as no surprise that control of Sandy Hook Lighthouse was a prime focus of both the British army and the colonial militias.

The patriots wanted to extinguish the flame of the beacon so the feared British Navy could not use it as a guiding light for entering the harbor. Just the same, the British did everything within their power to maintain control of the sentinel.

5

In addition, the enviable outlook capabilities provided by the tower's height enabled the British army to gain a spectacular panoramic view of the entire harbor and surrounding lands.

British troops would successfully hold Sandy Hook Lighthouse "hostage" throughout most of the Revolutionary War, except for one courageous incident in which a band of feisty patriots tried to stall a pending invasion of the great city by darkening and disabling the venerable sentinel. The New Jersey Lighthouse Society web site (www.njlhs.burlco.org) states that, "in early 1776 the British fleet was shortly expected to appear off New York City, prior to the invasion of that city. The New York Congress, on March 4, 1776, resolved to destroy the light so as not to aid the enemy. On March 6 instructions were issued to Major Malcolm to remove the lens and lamps in secret."

Major William Malcolm's daring efforts were successful as evidenced in a letter penned by Colonel George Taylor on March 12, 1776. According to the New Jersey Lighthouse Society web site, the letter stated, "received from Wm. Malcolm, eight

copper lamps, two tackle falls and blocks, three casks and a part of a cask of oil, being articles brought from the light-house on Sandy Hook." It didn't take long for the British fleet to realize that the guiding light atop Sandy Hook was extinguished as nightfall shrouded the entrance to the harbor under a cloak of darkness.

Furious about losing the lighthouse as a guiding light for their military use, the British hastily ordered

Photo by Bob Trapani, Jr.

Sandy Hook Lighthouse and keeper's house

a contingent of men to land at Sandy Hook and relight the beacon at once. Without use of the original equipment that Major Malcolm removed from the lighthouse during the raid, the British troops were forced to improvise and rig a set of makeshift lamps and reflectors to serve as the light source.

The New Jersey Lighthouse Society web site goes on to say, "this effort was apparently successful, because on June 1, 1776, the Americans again tried to douse the light, this time using a pair of six-pounders (cannon) mounted on several small boats under the command of Captain John Conover. The Americans succeeded in damaging the tower somewhat before being driven off by an approaching armed vessel."

Things are not always what they seem at face value, and in the case of Sandy Hook Lighthouse, nothing could be truer. The patriots thought that the sentinel was merely an invaluable guide for the powerful British Navy, but what they didn't realize was that the lighthouse was also a sentry of death for their fellow militiamen.

Prisoners' Crypt

The March 12, 1914 edition of the *Lincoln Daily News*, Nebraska, shed light on Sandy Hook's ghostly secret, stating that the British built and commissioned the lighthouse with a double purpose in mind. The newspaper account goes on to say, "it was intended to serve also as a military prison."

To the lighthouse enthusiast, this might seem like a preposterous statement—for nothing in the annals of American lighthouse history suggests a similar precedent. Yet as outrageous as it sounds that

Sandy Hook Lighthouse, the nation's oldest surviving guiding light

Photo by Bob Trapani, Jr.

a lighthouse could serve as a beacon for safe navigation and at the same time a dungeon for death and suffering, the unfathomable fact is true. Sandy Hook's massive foundation was, in effect, an eternal crypt holding the bones of those who chose to oppose the Royal Crown.

The *Lincoln Daily News* went on to verify this ghastly history, stating, "it was constructed with a dungeon underneath, and just 100 years later, in supplying a foundation for an iron stairway, evidence of its former use was made apparent through the discovery of a vault containing a human skeleton."

This horrifying dual-identity of Sandy Hook Lighthouse did not end with the findings of an unlikely "bridge" to the Great Divide. The newspaper account further described the sentinel's elaborate tomb of doom, saying, "This old lighthouse also had its secret underground passage, the entrance to which was barred by an iron door located in a nearby hillside. Then too, in this year of reconstruction, the holes that were made in the sides of the tower by cannon shots from British men-of-war were cemented."

Imagine if the lightkeeper, who spent many hours in the base of the light preparing his oil and other necessary equipment for the light source, had been made aware of Sandy Hook's frightening double identity? Do you think he would have thought it a refreshing experience to work in the cool base of the tower during summertime when the chilled atmosphere could have been easily interpreted as the hand of death itself touching his shoulder?

No doubt the keepers always thought they were alone in their work, but little did they know that a fallen patriot was "standing watch" with them, just underneath their feet.

Sandy Hook Lighthouse Facts and Figures

- Sandy Hook Lighthouse was constructed in 1764 and has the distinction of being the oldest operating lighthouse in America.
- When the lighthouse was built, it was a mere 500 yards from the end of the hook. Today, the lighthouse is 1.5 miles south of the hook thanks to the northward migration of sands along the coast.
- The tower is 103 feet tall, with a focal plane of 90 feet from sea.
- Sandy Hook Lighthouse retains its beautiful third order Fresnel lens and continues as an active aid to navigation. The lens shows a light emitting from a 1000-watt lamp, a beam that can be seen up to 19 nautical miles at sea.
- The light station resides in old Fort Hancock—both of which are now part of the Gateway National Recreation Area today. The United States Coast Guard transferred ownership of Sandy Hook Lighthouse to the National Park Service in 1996.

Photo by Bob Trapani, Jr.

Harbor of Refuge Lighthouse
Delaware

Bob Trapani, Jr.

History of Storms, Destruction and Death

F ew lighthouses along the entire Atlantic seaboard absorb more pounding from King Neptune's raging fury than Harbor of Refuge Lighthouse. Standing out in the Atlantic Ocean to mark the entrance to Delaware Bay and the National Harbor of Refuge Breakwater, this wave-swept sentinel possesses a storied history full of horrific storms, destruction and death.

Not long after the Federal government completed the 1.5 mile long stone breakwater in 1901 to safeguard shipping from the effects of the dreaded northeast gale, it became apparent that marking the wall with a light was going to be a war of attrition with the fierce elements of the Atlantic.

The United States Lighthouse Service first established a temporary beacon and fog bell on the south end of the National Harbor of Refuge Breakwater in 1902, but such efforts to mark the entrance to the harbor were short-lived. One year later the seas would rise up on the shoulders of a great hurricane to swallow the beacon and bell—sending both to an eternal watery grave.

The warning signals were not the only casualties of the storm, as the maelstrom's sweeping havoc refused to distinguish the difference between inanimate objects and human lives.

Shipwrecks and Storms

The headlines in the September 17, 1903, *Coshocton Daily Age* newspaper read, "Storm King Sweeps Whole Atlantic Coast . . . Mountain Waves Crash Ships Like Shells—Lives Lost." The account went on to say, "The southern storm which had been coming up the Atlantic coast for several days struck the

Delaware capes with almost cyclonic force, and as a result at least five lives were lost."

The five lives lost to the hurricane happened to be in the same area where the temporary beacon and fog bell were washed overboard on the end of the massive stone breakwater. Though the storm was short-lived in duration at four hours, it packed overwhelming power with winds clocked at 85 miles per hour and rain that fell in torrents.

Trying to ride out the storm was the ill-fated wooden schooner *Hattie A. Marsh*, hailing from Painters Point, Maine, and carrying a cargo of paving stones. Captain J. B. Mehaffey tried desperately to keep his ship afloat and away from the ravaging effects of the razor-sharp stone breakwater but his efforts proved fruitless.

The *Coshocton Daily Age* went on to report, "The Captain tried to anchor but the anchors did not hold, and the schooner with her dead weight of stones was dashed on the rocks of the Harbor of Refuge. The steam pilot boat *Philadelphia* went to the rescue, but succeeded in saving only mate Norman Campbell and one seaman. Captain Mehaffey and four sailors were lost."

The U.S. Lighthouse Service would re-establish a temporary beacon and fog bell at the site until a lighthouse could be built, but the hurricane of 1903 served notice of the sea's violence, which would forever be linked to the history of the Harbor of Refuge Light Station.

Photo courtesy of U.S. Coast Guard

The original lighthouse was also known as the Belle of the Bay.

'Belle of the Bay'

On November 20, 1908, the original Harbor of Refuge Lighthouse was lit for the first time as it sent out a flashing white light every 12 seconds from a fourth order Fresnel lens over the horizon. Mariners described the new lighthouse as the "Belle of the Bay" for its ornate hexagonal appearance, but for all its aesthetics, its construction was ill suited for such a remote and dangerous location. Despite a height of 52-feet, the structure could not stand above harrowing storm seas.

Keeper Jack Hill of the nearby Delaware Breakwater East End Lighthouse recounted the terrific waves that pounded the "Belle of the Bay," saying, "I have seen it (seas) hit Harbor of Refuge so hard that the waves would go as high as the top of the tower." Hill added, "From Delaware Breakwater you could hardly tell for a fraction of a second, that there was a lighthouse there."

Two immense storms in 1918 and 1920 each moved Harbor of Refuge Lighthouse off its foundation roughly two inches, to the agonizing dismay of it keepers. In fact, Keeper Robert Taylor documented the horror of the tempests in the station's daily log. "April 10 & 11, 1918: We had a storm wind, N.E. gale did considerable damage to this station's storehouse roof. Broken lighthouse foundation shifted the big light about 2 inches on the foundation."

Two years later, Keeper Taylor recorded even more damage to the light station, stating, "February 3, 4 & 5, 1920: We had a N.E. storm and a gale did some damage here. The old house, the bell and the boat davit and the rowboat, water tanks, and in fact, all that was in the house, washed overboard with the house. One barrel of oil, lots of tools, also fog signal gears. It washed everything off the dock. The wind and high sea, and also moved the big lighthouse about 2 inches on its foundation. And also torn away a large portion of the platform. And breaking in the engine room and the sea wash inside and could not get out. No water to drink."

The incredible pounding from these two storms rendered Harbor of Refuge Lighthouse nearly uninhabitable, but it would be another six years before the United States Lighthouse Service would condemn the structure. On April 12, 1926, Keeper Robert Taylor extinguished the light for the final time as contractors began the process of dismantling the storm-battered sentinel.

The April 12th date is significant, for on the very next day—April 13, 1926—the mighty Cape Henlopen Lighthouse lost its battle with erosion as fell into the sea due to an undermined sandy foundation. Thus, on back to back days, the state of Delaware lost two historic lighthouses.

By November 15, 1926, a new and stout Harbor of Refuge Lighthouse was completed. The cast-iron sentinel was taller, stronger and better suited than its predecessor to take on the daunting challenge of standing up to King Neptune. Two-and-a-half years later, the lighthouse was to be tested by a tempest of terrifying strength. Keeper Robert Taylor no doubt felt more secure in the new cast-iron sentinel as opposed to the previous wooden superstructure, but that did not stop him from fretting about the power of the sea at this exposed location.

Taylor recorded the effects of the April 14-16, 1929, storm in his daily log, stating, "It was blowing about 78 mph, it was pretty bad on Monday night 15th. The lighthouse shook bad. We had a job to keep the light working, the house shook so. What we need is stone put on the northeast side to break the sea up before it hits the house for we know what the sea does around here. No one (who has) never saw it does not realize what it is around here in a storm. All the damage it done here, it busted the row-boat No. 93 all to pieces . . . . We could not get down on the dock from Monday morning until Tuesday afternoon for the sea was washing over the top of the dock about 6 feet on the level."

'Storm of the Century'

Mother Nature would continue to lash at Harbor of Refuge Lighthouse over the next 33 years, including a visit by Hurricane Dona in 1960, which shattered a window on the main deck of the structure with a rogue wave. But the one storm that will live on in infamy at Harbor of Refuge Light Station is the great, unnamed storm of March 6-8, 1962—a tempest that would eventually be classified as Delaware's "Storm of the Century."

Stephen Jones, former Harbor of Refuge lightkeeper, has captured the impact and emotion of this storm in his maritime classic, entitled *Harbor of Refuge*, and in firsthand accounts shared during two return visits to the offshore sentinel in 2002 and 2004.

Keeper Jones recalled that there was no indication whatsoever that he and his comrades were about to experience storm-tossed chaos of immense proportions the day before the tempest's arrival off the Delaware capes.

The day "was clear and surprisingly warm," said Jones, as the men took advantage of the favorable temperatures to get in some painting within the berthing areas of the lighthouse. After dinner on the night of March 5th, Jones turned in for what he thought would be a restful sleep. But after dozing off for about an hour, the first in a chain of unnerving events occurred—and would continue unabated for the next 72 hours.

The agitated seas were slowly being whipped into frenzy. And in the process, the wave action slamming against the caisson base of the lighthouse woke Keeper Jones from his sleep as his bed periodically shook. Brushing off this disturbing trend, Jones fell back to sleep before suddenly being awakened by a frantic comrade who flipped on the lights in the berthing area.

Keeper Jones quickly rose from his bed in dazed fashion and placed his feet in icy water that covered the hardwood floors of the sleeping quarters. For the next half-hour, the three-man crew worked to board up a window on the second level that was shattered by a high-rising rogue wave. The sea also poured down into the lower level of the structure, shorting out the radio—the only means of communicating with the outside world.

Day two of the storm was ushered in following a wild and sleepless night, yet as keeper Jones recalled, "Morning did not come. Time did pass, measured by dripping, erased by swaying; and somewhere in the swaying came a cold light out of the east."

A random glance through a salt-sprayed windowpane revealed a horrifying sight looming from the east that Jones described as "such a mass of water as I'd not

Photo by Bob Trapani, Jr.

Former keeper Stephen Jones shares a story while visiting Harbor of Refuge Lighthouse, where he worked during the 1960s.

thought possible. I don't know why there should have seemed to be so much of it. I certainly could see no farther than usual, and there were no landmarks out that way to be now covered, but there it was volume."

The mountainous seas now enveloping the lighthouse were violently assaulting the cast-iron caisson structure with such force that the tower was shuddering ceaselessly. Furniture was "walking" across the floor. Canned goods were falling from the pantry shelves. Eventually, even the lights inside the structure went out, plunging the Coast Guard crew into a world of uncertain darkness.

To make matters worse, the indomitable breakwater—the only solid land, would vanish beneath a seething ocean for the duration of the storm.

As much as they tried to block out thoughts of doom, the prospect of the lighthouse failing to stand firm against such cataclysmic seas and thoughts of their own mortality no doubt crept into the minds of the keepers as the tower continued to shake and moan under the strain of seas gone mad.

The "Storm of the Century" finally loosened its terrifying grip upon Delaware's coast and Harbor of Refuge Lighthouse by the end of the 8th day of March 1962, but not before wreaking unprecedented havoc on the defenseless barrier beaches and shore towns.

The tempest was described as a "slow-moving late-winter coastal storm of unusual development, composition and behavior," by meteorological sources. The force of devastation was enacted by winds of 60 miles per hour, waves as high as 20 to 40 feet coming ashore and five terribly destructive high tides—two being over nine feet above normal.

When asked if he and his fellow lightkeepers had an idea of the magnitude of the northeast storm, Jones replied, "No, it wasn't like there was a voice from out of the blue telling us: 'THIS is the storm of the century. . . . It took 40 years to pass for us to learn of that distinction."

Harbor of Refuge Lighthouse Facts and Figures

•   The Federal government constructed the National Harbor of Refuge Breakwater over a period of four years, from 1897 to 1901, to safeguard shipping from storms such the fierce winter nor'easters. The stone wall is 1.5-miles in length and cost the government two million dollars to construct.

• The first lighthouse was established atop the south end of the National Harbor of Refuge Breakwater on November 20, 1908. The superstructure was hexagonal in shape and constructed of wood, standing 52 feet above the sea.

• Storm damage caused the demise of the original lighthouse, and a new sentinel was built and completed on November 15, 1926. The new lighthouse was constructed of cast-iron and stands 76-feet above the sea.

• Harbor of Refuge Lighthouse was automated in 1973 as the Coast Guard removed the beacon's last resident personnel in December of that year. The lighthouse continues to serve mariners in the 21st century with its guiding light and is maintained by USCG Aids to Navigation Team, Cape May, New Jersey.

• The non-profit Delaware River & Bay Lighthouse Foundation signed a 20-year historic lease with the United States Coast Guard on April 1, 2002, to care for Harbor of Refuge Lighthouse. On September 30, 2004, the U.S. Department of the Interior granted the DRBLHF ownership of the lighthouse under the guidelines of the National Historic Lighthouse Preservation Act 2000.

• Harbor of Refuge Lighthouse made history by becoming the first mid-Atlantic offshore lighthouse to be made accessible to the general public in 2003. Today, the general public can "walk in the steps of the keeper" at Harbor of Refuge and learn about the rich history of Delaware Bay lights and Lewes Harbor during regularly scheduled seasonal tours.

To learn more about the efforts of the Delaware River & Bay Lighthouse Foundation to save and interpret the region's lighthouse heritage, visit its web site at www.delawarebaylights.org

Delaware River & Bay Lighthouse Foundation
P.O. Box 708
Lewes, DE 19958
(302) 644-7046

Photo by Bob Trapani, Jr.

Cape May Lighthouse
New Jersey

Blinded by the Light

I n his book *Sentinel of the Jersey Cape*, author John Bailey
eloquently describes the beacon at Cape May Point, saying,
"Behold the Cape May Lighthouse. She stands there so silent-
ly and aloof that we find it difficult to fathom her age and the
epochs that have swirled about her base."

From great Atlantic storms that have played out on turbulent
seascapes beneath its guiding beam to ceaseless erosion that has
starkly reshaped the southern cape of New Jersey, Cape May
Lighthouse has witnessed a plethora of historic moments over a
164 year period. As Mr. Bailey states, much of this rich history has
occurred at the foot of the lighthouse, but on occasion, noteworthy
phenomena have played out in the air—145 feet above ground.

Cape May Lighthouse has long been one of sentinels on the
Atlantic seaboard that unexplainably lures confused birds into its
entrancing beam of light.

"Lighthouses that lie along great migration routes are especially
susceptible," said renowned lighthouse author Elinor De Wire.
"Almost all lighthouse logbooks mention these tragic occurrences
from time to time, some with emotion, others as if such events
were as natural as the combers kissing the beach."

The keepers' nonchalant reaction to fowl crashing into the
Cape May Lighthouse was made evident by a news reporter talk-
ing to one of the men at the light station back in 1905.

Fowling Up the Light

The *Grand Rapids Tribune* of Wisconsin picked up on a
story where an astounded reporter accompanied one of the
lightkeepers—either Head Keeper Caleb S. Woolson, 1st Assistant
Edward Hughes or 2nd Assistant J.S. Pusey—on a climb up the

199 steps inside the sentinel to the watchroom area high above the ground.

During the reporter's evening visit, a hard-striking "thud" took the visitor by surprise as he chatted with the keeper on night watch. The source of the unexpected sound was the lantern room where netting surrounded the glass panes protecting the powerful first order Fresnel lens rotating inside. The light was diligently sending out a white flashing beam, once every 30 seconds, over the Atlantic Ocean and entrance to the Delaware Bay.

The 12-foot tall lantern might have been an impressive crown to the 157-foot, 6-inch tower, but to airborne birds or fowl, the top of the lighthouse was certain death in the sky. Whether being blinded by the lantern's light or mistaking it for the sun, the results of flying straight into the irresistible beam proved deadly more often than not.

Stopping his candid conversation with the news reporter in midstream, the keeper on watch casually walked outside to confirm what he already suspected. When the keeper returned from his inspection of the balcony area he totted a dead bird in hand. "A mud hen," said the night watch. "Sometimes we get five or six in a night. Often we find robins and ducks dead on the balcony."

The news reporter was enchanted by the life of a lightkeeper and commented to the night watch, "It's a fine life you lead here."

Taking the opening without missing a beat, the keeper switched the conversation from birds crashing into Cape May Lighthouse to something that was personally bothersome. "Yes; if it wasn't for the oil—the six gallons of oil that the light burns nightly," said the night watch.

Apparently the task of carting heavy containers of oil up the plethora of stairs each day proved frustrating enough for this particular keeper, that he relished the rare opportunity to vent his displeasure.

"The government won't give us any machinery to hoist it up with. Consequently every day I must carry the whole six gallons up these 217 steps (from ground level to the top of the light). That's hard on the heart."

The visitor commented that it might be easier just to rig up a rope and pulley arrangement outside the lantern room and lift the cumbersome containers of oil in that fashion.

The keeper shook his head in disagreement, saying, "It ain't allowed. In every oil-burning lighthouse the attendants must carry up the oil by hand. It does seem . . . ."

Without warning, the keeper's lament was interrupted in midstream by another eerie plopping sound. Indifferent to the dilemma, the news reporter noted that the keeper simply, "slipped out to get another mud hen."

> "The sea-bird wheeling round it, with the din
> Of wings and winds and solitary cries,
> Blinded and maddened by the light within,
> Dashes himself against the glare, and dies."
> —*Henry Wadsworth Longfellow*

Cape May Lighthouse Facts and Figures

- The lighthouse tower is 157 feet 6 inches tall, from the ground line to the ventilator ball on top.
- There are 218 steps from the ground to the top, with 199 steps in the tower's cast iron spiral staircase.
- The Cape May Lighthouse was built in 1859, and is the third known lighthouse to be built at Cape May Point. The first was built in 1823; the second in 1847. The exact locations of the first two lighthouses are now under water due to erosion.
- The Coast Guard continues to operate the light as an active aid to navigation. The light is visible 24 miles out at sea and flashes every 15 seconds.
- The State of New Jersey owns the Lighthouse, but the Coast Guard maintains the beacon apparatus and emergency generator. The Mid-Atlantic Center for the Arts (MAC) in Cape May leases the lighthouse from the State with the mission of restoring the structure and operating it as a historic site.

To learn more about the Mid-Atlantic Center for the Arts and Cape May Lighthouse, visit the web site at www.capemaymac.org (from which this information was secured)

Mid-Atlantic Center for the Arts
1048 Washington Street
P.O. Box 340
Cape May, NJ 08204
(609)-884-5404 or (800)-275-4278

Photo by Bob Trapani, Jr.

Fourteen Foot Bank Lighthouse
Delaware

Bob Trapani, Jr.

House of Horrors

Fourteen Foot Bank and Joe Flogger shoals were menacing dangers to 18th- and 19th-century shipping on the Delaware Bay until the federal government established a lightship to mark the shallow-water hazards in 1876. This improvement for navigation was highly valued by the maritime community throughout the year except for the most critical of times—winter.

During the 10-year period between 1876 and 1886, lightships simply could not hold their position in the face of an onslaught of running ice floes. When mariners desperately needed the guiding light the most to safeguard them from the deadly shoals, the lightship was invariably either running for cover or being carried away against its will by the overpowering grasp of ice being chased down river by the ebb tide.

Congress finally authorized the United States Lighthouse Service to deploy an expensive new technology that could establish a lighthouse on the unpredictable site in place of the ineffective lightship. Using the pneumatic process, contractors imbedded a caisson into the seabed, and from there, constructed an impressive cast-iron Victorian superstructure. By 1887, Fourteen Foot Bank Lighthouse sent out its first beam of light over Delaware Bay. Though the presence of this water-locked beacon did not totally prevent ships from wrecking on the treacherous shoals, its benefit to sea borne commerce was huge.

Over the years Fourteen Foot Bank Lighthouse is credited with saving the lives of many mariners with its guiding beam. Unfortunately, the same cannot be said for one of the men who helped tend the flame high atop the beacon.

Agonizing accident

Lewis Robinson of Lewes, Delaware, was a keeper at the lighthouse during 1910 when he suffered an accident that would haunt him the rest of his brief life. It seems that one of the other keepers inadvertently left the trapdoor to the caisson basement open when an unsuspecting Robinson accidentally fell through. In an instant, the keeper dropped 20 feet and slammed against the dark concrete floor of the basement in bone-rattling fashion. Robinson screamed out to his fellow comrade, who was on duty with him, for help. By the time the other keeper made his way to Robinson's aid, it was apparent that professional medical care would be necessary.

Keeper Robinson suffered multiple bruises from the fall but the most painful injury he sustained was a broken ankle. Normally people who suffer this type of injury immediately seek a physician's care—which was what keeper Robinson desperately desired, but one small problem existed.

Fourteen Foot Bank Lighthouse is located a few miles offshore from the nearest shore town of Bowers Beach, Delaware. The healthy keeper tried to send signals of distress but evidently they were not understood or went unheeded by passing commercial ships.

Adding to the keeper's plight was the fact that since it was wintertime, the normal presence of recreational fishermen bobbing up and down near the lighthouse in their personal craft try-

Photo by Bob Trapani, Jr.

Fourteen Foot Bank Lighthouse, where keeper Robinson suffered a horrifying fall

ing to catch some of the bounty of the bay was but a distant summer memory.

A Maryland newspaper stated at the time that, "vessels were signaled while the man lay in pain, but owing to the high wind and seas, no communication was possible." Since the lighthouse was established to warn ships of the deadly shoals it presided over, vessels naturally stayed far off the area – making it near impossible for someone to notice the keeper's meager signals of distress over an expansive bay.

Unable to get off the lighthouse, keeper Robinson spent the next two weeks suffering immense agony, all the while unable to eat or drink very much owing to the unceasing pain. His fellow comrade did everything he could to make Robinson as comfortable as possible, but all to no avail.

Finally, head keeper Wilson returned to Fourteen Foot Bank Light from his shore leave two weeks later to find his assistant living a torturous nightmare that seemed to have no end. At that point, the crew lowered injured keeper Robinson down from the lighthouse—a maneuver that only increased the man's suffering as each movement and twist proved excruciating. Once aboard the boat Robinson had to endure further anguish from the bouncing and pounding of the waterborne craft on his journey back to Lewes.

Eventually his awful ordeal of being trapped inside the house of horrors at Fourteen Foot Bank Lighthouse ended when he arrived in town and was finally able to see a physician for his shattered ankle.

Photo by Bob Trapani, Jr.

Before indoor plumbing, all Delaware Bay lighthouses were provided with an outdoor privy—not the most pleasant experience when icy winds were swirling on the bay.

Returning to the scene

After a period of healing, keeper Robinson returned to the source of his nightmare—the lighthouse. Apparently, the whole experience scarred Robinson deeper than anyone could have surmised, because though he tended to his duties as lightkeeper without fail upon his return, his emotions were indubitably stirred to the depths of despair.

Six months had not quite come to pass before the dark shadows that continually haunted keeper Robinson since his ankle debacle finally overwhelmed his will to live. On June 11, 1911, two keepers were busy working in the caisson basement when they were startled by the terrifying screams of Robinson, who was alone topside.

Scrambling up to the room that was the source of the spine-tingling shrieking, the two keepers were aghast at what they had discovered.

The *Trenton Evening Times* described the horrid scene, saying that the keepers watched Robinson "die in great agony after he had confessed and expressed remorse for the act."

Evidently keeper Robinson decided to end whatever mental and physical suffering he was enduring by committing suicide. Rather than using a weapon, Robinson chose to drink carbolic acid and subsequently died an excruciatingly

Photo by Bob Trapani, Jr.

A fixed fourth order Fresnel lens, which was used at Fourteen Foot Bank Lighthouse from the late-1800s through the mid-1990s, is on display inside the Cannonball House in Lewes, Del.

slow and painful death—even more horrendous than his terrible ankle ordeal only months earlier.

Unable to leave Fourteen Foot Bank Lighthouse unattended, one of the two remaining lightkeepers was forced to stay behind and contemplate the frightening scene over and over as he tended the light each night. In the meantime, his fellow comrade rowed a hard pull over the bay to Lewes in a dory with the lifeless corpse of Robinson as his only "company."

The *Trenton Evening Times* entitled Robinson's fateful ordeal as a "Tragedy in a Lighthouse." The newspaper went on to convey to their readers a summation of the keeper's actions by stating, "it is thought by many here that the sufferings he endured while ill affected his mind, and that it led him to commit the rash deed."

Fourteen Foot Bank Lighthouse Facts and Figures

• The lighthouse was completed in 1887 and shows a light 59 feet above sea level that can be seen 12 nautical miles.
• Once equipped with a fourth order Fresnel lens, today Fourteen Foot Bank Lighthouse has a modern 300mm acrylic optic and is maintained by the United States Coast Guard Aids to Navigation Team, Cape May, New Jersey.
• Fourteen Foot Bank Lighthouse has the distinction of being the first beacon in America to be constructed with the pneumatic process.
• The fourth order Fresnel lens from Fourteen Foot Bank Lighthouse resides in Lewes, Delaware, and is on display inside the Cannonball House on Front Street. To learn more about Cannonball House, which is part of the Lewes Historical Society, visit the web site at www.historiclewes.org

Photo by Bob Trapani, Jr.

Miah Maull Shoal Lighthouse
New Jersey

Bob Trapani, Jr.

Keepers' Secret of the Crying Wall

There is something about Miah Maull Shoal Lighthouse that exudes the mysterious. Rising 59 feet above the water in the middle of the Delaware Bay, this red caisson sentinel has spent the last 92 years warning mariners of the deadly shoal by the same name that it presides over. Yet it's what occurred more than a century prior at the site that seems to haunt the light station to this very day.

The sandy shoal, lurking a mere 13 feet below the water in some places, was named after Nehemiah Maull who shipwrecked and drowned on this despicable hazard in 1780 while in route to England to lay claim to his share of a family fortune.

Coastguardsmen servicing the automated sentinel to this day contend that Miah Maull Shoal Lighthouse is haunted, saying that each visit to the water-locked site simply "gives them the creeps."

If only they knew of the legend that had been passed down for decades from lightkeeper to lightkeeper before technology banished human presence from the lighthouse. In the 30-plus years since resident personnel were removed from Miah Maull, the "keepers' secret" has been mostly lost to the pages of history, but not entirely forgotten.

Keepers' Secret

Whether the keepers feared reprisal for their "secret" or did not want to be considered to have lost their minds, the legend of the "Crying Wall" remained largely untold outside the small circle of Delaware Bay lightkeepers.

Ever since its construction many of Miah Maull's keepers and their assistants witnessed a mysterious seepage in one specific

29

spot on the wall inside the first floor of the lighthouse. Strangely, this eerie phenomenon never occurred in summer's heat, but rather during wintertime when "Old Man Winter" possessed a firm stranglehold on the expansive bay. Further adding to the intrigue was the fact that a storm had to be brewing on the horizon for the wall to begin sweating.

Though the diameter of the first level of Miah Maull Shoal Lighthouse is approximately 26 feet, the "Crying Wall" chose to only occupy an area about 6 feet in height and a few feet wide. Initially, many lightkeepers made the mistake of believing that the wall was merely exhibiting a sweating condition due to the humidity present in the structure or condensation brought about by changes in temperatures within the brick-lined wall. Before long, however, each keeper realized his "logical" assessment of an unexplainable situation was hardly adequate due to the fact that the remainder of the interior wall was not suffering from the same condition.

The sight of the wall's extraordinary appearance during times of a looming storm frightened each of the keepers. For the more the men peered at the seepage, the more the wall would run with mysterious water. Finally, one unidentified lightkeeper decided to investigate this baffling situation more closely. He later confided to his comrade that, "Water would start to drip and roll down the wall the closer I got. I felt the wall with my hands in order to try and see where it was coming from. It was then that I heard the crying."

Sobbing Sounds

Upon hearing the sobbing sound, the keeper quickly stepped back in fright. With his heart racing at an uncontrollable rate, he tried to regain his composure before inching ever so closely again for another curious listen. The crying was only coming from the wet parts of the wall. Terrified, yet determined to prove he wasn't hearing things, the keeper placed his ear against the wall. Just like the previous moment, the sobbing sounds emitted from the unfathomable seepage. This caused the keeper to comment, "the more the wall would 'cry,' the more 'tears' fell."

Many of the lighthouse keepers believed the crying was the spirit of Nehemiah Maull who drowned at the site in the late

18th century, while others contended that quite possibly the sound was that of his grieving wife. Strangely, once the keepers would accept the "Crying Wall" as part of lighthouse life, it would weep for a while then stop. Another keeper noted that it was "almost like a person in mourning." He said we simply "stood back and let them mourn in their own time."

Though whoever chooses to mourn, their sorrow never seems to have ended, for the phenomenon spanned the era of the light station being manned—and apparently, the haunted atmosphere has continued into the age of automation.

Today Miah Maull Shoal Lighthouse continues to stand silent sentinel as it shines a guiding light to ships transiting the main channel of Delaware Bay. The beacon is devoid of all human presence on a regular basis but evidently not entirely unoccupied.

Miah Maull Shoal Lighthouse Facts and Figures

• Construction of the lighthouse began at Miah Maull Shoal in June, 1908, while a temporary light was exhibited during the construction process on September 13, 1909.

• The lighthouse was completed and first shown a permanent light from its lantern room on February 20, 1913.

• The lighthouse stands 59 feet tall.

• The nearest town to the offshore lighthouse is Fortescue, New Jersey, some 7 miles in distance across the bay to shore.

• The lighthouse was originally painted brown, but sometime around 1941, the Coast Guard changed the color of the super-structure to red.

• The lighthouse marks Miah Maull Shoal, which is approximately 800 yards wide and 3,000 feet in length.

• The lighthouse remains an active aid to navigation and is maintained by the United States Coast Guard Aids to Navigation, Cape May, New Jersey.

Port Mahon Lighthouse
Delaware

Bob Trapani, Jr.

Captain McGowan's Schooner of Fiery Death

The golden brown phragmites of Port Mahon are a striking sight. Towering eight to 12 feet above the marshland, clusters of reeds dance in concert to the choreography set forth by the winds of Delaware Bay. And for many decades in their swaying murmur, a bay legend has remained—a nearly lost secret, hidden in the bosom of this forsaken morass.

Today, at the edge of this eroding mire stands 16 eerie looking pilings, oozing rust and surrounded by the victorious tides of the bay. The immovable cast iron pilings are a ghostly reminder of a bygone light station absorbed into the pages of history.

Though up to five different lighthouses stood sentinel at Mahon River since 1831, it is the last lighthouse constructed in 1903 that remains forever tied to the mysterious sight of a "burning schooner" and the cries of its captain on the moonlit waters of the Delaware Bay.

The last Mahon River Lighthouse was a simple but charming white, square, two-story building placed atop the stout shoulders of the 16 lonely pilings. At one time, in this quaint home, after escaping the icy winds of the bay, oystermen would periodically pay a visit.

And as the night wore on, they latched the door, ensuring that only those who might understand the shadowy unknowns of Delaware Bay were within earshot. Only then would the oystermen tell the lightkeeper and his family their frightening tale—one they claimed occurred time and again, not far off the point from where the lighthouse stood. And with each retelling of the terrifying mystery, an eerie hush fell over all who were present.

Telling Terrifying Bay Tales

Dorothy Lynch, daughter of Mahon River Lighthouse keeper Irvin Lynch, Sr., recalled the scene, saying, "Sometimes the oystermen would come in to have a cup of coffee or just to talk. I always stayed at the kitchen table so I could hear their stories, though they mostly talked about the day on the water and how good their harvest of oysters had been. Sometimes, though, they'd have some really good stories to tell."

Only when the conversation between the oystermen and the lightkeeper began to wander down the road of all things unexplained would the subject of the "burning schooner" be broached. Such legends prove intriguing when recounted by one person, but they become irresistible when a group of people admit to experiencing the same ghostly aberration.

Photo courtesy of Penny Czerwinski

"Quite a few of the oystermen told a similar story at different times," said Dorothy. Each man would cite a similar setting that was spawned on with the sun being chased from the western sky by the dark realm of nightfall.

Furthermore, the "burning schooner" apparently did not choose to ply the blackened waters of the Delaware Bay without the presence of a milky white backdrop that could shed a ghostly light on its eternal voyage.

The men insisted that it is only during periods of a near or

Dorothy Lynch, daughter of a lighthouse keeper, listened to local watermen share tales of the river and bay.

full moon when the phantom schooner ablaze is beckoned to
ride again in grisly fashion. Even the normally agitated seas of a
fickle bay went flat during such cadaverous transits.

"The water on the bay would be real still, hardly a ripple,"
said Dorothy. "Some of the oystermen said they'd hear a sound
off in the distance, like that of people screaming. When they
would look towards the direction of the sound they'd see a
shape like an old schooner, but misty in appearance. The men
said they thought they were seeing things and would rub their
eyes and look again. The schooner would become real clear—
just like it was right there."

As if the ghastly screams aboard the ship weren't enough,
the vessel itself even seemed to be bemoaning its own death
knell as well.

"The oystermen would hear the cracking and moaning
sound of a ship when it started to sink," said Dorothy. "The
whole thing would go up in flames." To a man, each person
knew this appalling scene should not just have appeared out of
thin air, for what rationale could be applied to its being.
Nonetheless, the oystermen knew what they saw—and no
amount of logic could repel the horrifying sight or its impact on
their senses. Dorothy recalled the men saying that "they could
actually feel the heat of the fire on their faces, but then they saw
the worst part of it."

Port Mahon Lighthouse during its active years

Photo courtesy of U.S. Coast Guard

What the local oystermen were actually viewing was the lurid legend of Captain Joshua McGowan, known all too well in the Port Mahon and nearby Little Creek locale. Scant accounts cut to the bone, state that the silhouetted corpse of Captain McGowan dangles from the bowsprit of his schooner thanks to an enraged member of his crew. Apparently, Captain McGowan became romantically involved with the daughter of one of Delaware's governors in the early 1800s. According to legend, a jealous crew member killed his captain and tied the dead body to the bowsprit of the ill-fated schooner before setting it ablaze.

Impaled on the Bowsprit

Dorothy recalled standing quietly in the kitchen of Port Mahon Lighthouse, hearing the oystermen recounting this most horrid tale—a story that sounds as if it comes straight from the crypt of Davey Jones. She quoted the men, saying, "impaled on the bowsprit was a man made visible by the light of fire—his face aglow in the color orange. The fire was so bright that it reflected off the bay, making it hard to tell where the flames stopped on the water."

Oystermen are a hearty lot not generally prone to spinning spectacular seaborne tales and lore, which makes the "burning schooner" legend quite intriguing. As Dorothy observed, "These

Photo by Bob Trapani, Jr.

Pilings are all that remain of the Port Mahon Lighthouse.

oystermen were a tough breed and not much bothered them, but they said the sight was so gruesome that most of them would look away. Some said the ship sank while others said it just faded away. The men all said they didn't dare tell many people about the haunting sight because others might think they were crazy. They'd tell us because we were lighthouse folks and we knew there could be some strange things out in that water."

The Port Mahon Lighthouse served as an active aid to navigation until the 1950s when its duties were shifted to a nearby modern skeletal tower. Unmanned, the lighthouse slowly marched toward its demise. By 1984 and only a shell of its former glory, the historic Port Mahon Lighthouse was completely destroyed by fire at the hands of vandals, leaving only the 16 ghostly cast-iron pilings as a lasting memorial to its service. One wonders if Captain McGowan sailed once more that fateful evening to mourn the loss of an "old friend" as the lighthouse slipped into oblivion to join him in the lore of Delaware Bay.

Port Mahon Lighthouse Facts and Figures

•   Up to five different lighthouses have resided at Mahon River over the years (1831, 1839, 1861, 1875 and 1903).
•   The last lighthouse at Mahon River or Port Mahon was completed in 1903 and lit for the first time on June 25, 1903.
•   The lighthouse was equipped with a fourth order Fresnel lens that showed a light 38 feet above mean high water.
•   Port Mahon Lighthouse was automated in 1939 and remained active until 1955 when the light was removed from the historic building and established on a modern skeletal tower.
•   The lighthouse was placed in the National Register of Historic Places in 1976.
•   General Services Administration declared the lighthouse excess property in 1982 and subsequently sold the building to Delaware Storage and Pipeline Company.
•   The wooden lighthouse was destroyed by fire on December 29, 1984.

Photo by Ann-Marie Trapani

Barnegat Lighthouse
New Jersey

Felines Commandeer Light Station Grounds

S ituated in the Irish Sea, halfway between Liverpool, England and Belfast, Ireland, is the Isle of Man. Despite the island's tiny size—which is a mere 221 square miles (32 miles long and 13 miles wide)—a world-renowned breed of cats without tails known as Manx hail from the Isle of Man.

Though many legends persist as to how the tailless breed arrived on the island, one account suggests that a doomed Spanish galleon shipwrecked near the coast during the 16th century at a place called Spanish Rock. The ship was carrying a cargo from the Far East and a number of tailless cats before King Neptune claimed the vessel for his own.

The legend goes on to say that many of the cats managed to survive the shipwreck, either swimming or riding the waves on broken pieces of the vessel to shore. Once the cats scrambled from the clutches of the sea, they eventually established a colony on the Isle of Man. If the Spanish galleon tale is true and the Manx cat indeed did arrive on the Isle of Man aboard the driftwood of a shipwreck, then history was doomed to repeat itself.

Shipwreck Survivors

During the middle 1800s, a terrifying nor'easter was pounding the New Jersey coast with incredible force, wreaking havoc with sailing ships traversing the turbulent Atlantic. One unidentified vessel was unable to fight against the mountainous seas and horrific winds, eventually "giving up the ghost" on the beach near the 1859 red and white Barnegat Lighthouse. Though the seas unmercifully splintered the wooden ship into oblivion, the crew and its cargo managed to escape their dance with fate.

Keeper Joshua H. Reeves, who tended the light at Barnegat from 1875 to 1885, vividly recalled the details of the shipwreck that were passed down from previous keepers of the light known as Old Barney. Reeves was quoted in the April 25, 1899, edition of the *Daily Republican* newspaper from Illinois as saying, "In addition to her crew, the ship carried a score or more of Manx cats, which were being carried from the Isle of Man to New York. Nearly all the cats succeeded in reaching the shore. They took to the woods and no effect was ever made to reclaim them."

The normal temperament of the Manx cat is found to be obedient, quiet and affectionate—much like a dog, but whether it was the long ride across the Atlantic, trauma suffered from the shipwreck or being rebuffed by humans at the lighthouse, Barnegat's marooned felines grew tough and independent.

Keeper Reeves provided some insight into the cat's first encounter with rejection when he commented, "for a while these tailless animals loitered around the lighthouse in search of food but as the keeper had no liking for so numerous a family of cats he drove them away. When I took charge of the lighthouse the cats had become wild, and while I could approach within a short distance of them, they would not allow themselves to be caught. The woods were full of cats."

Taste for Surf and Turf

Finding a home in the thick underbrush of the sand dunes, the colony of Manx cats soon ruled the beach around the light station with an iron claw. Keeper Reeves remembered there was no shortage of sustenance for the breed, saying, "They found plenty of food by preying on the birds that lived in great numbers in the woods. Rabbits, which were plentiful on the island before the cats were cast ashore, were soon killed or driven away, for they were no match for their feline antagonists." The cats soon demonstrated that they also appreciated "surf and turf" when it came to diversifying their diet as they learned how to become proficient at dining on the bounty of the sea.

"The cats even became expert fishers," said keeper Reeves. "I have often watched them at work. In the spring and fall of the year large schools of fish swim about in the surf and these gave the cats many a feast. As the breakers drove the fish upon the beach, into a few inches of water, the cats would rush into the surf and inserting their claws in the sides of the half-stranded fish, would devour them."

Eventually, United States Life-Saving Service surfmen stationed on the island at Barnegat brought domesticated cats to live with them. It didn't take long for the cats from the mainland to get acquainted with their rough and tumble counterparts, and in fact, some of the domestic cats even joined the wild colony.

Keeper Reeves recalled the dismaying results of this bonding, saying, "There soon were tailless cats, cats with half a tail and cats with the regulation tail. The animals thrived and soon became a nuisance. In the thick underbrush of the woods they raised large litters of young ones."

In an effort to control the troublesome wild cats, locals staged cat-hunting parties that attracted sportsmen from the mainland. The hunts became popular and many cats were sent to a sandy grave. In spite of efforts to kill-off the Manx colony, they survived and continued to multiply.In the 1902 book entitled, *The Book of the Cat*, by Frances Simpson, the author described the Manx breed, commenting, "These quaint cats are rapidly and surely coming into notice in the fancy as a breed. They are intelligent and affectionate, and, I believe, splendid sporting cats."

If only the author had been aware of just how splendid of a sporting cat the Manx were on Barnegat Island, the book might have required another chapter to recount their amazing exploits in the sand dunes near Old Barney.

Barnegat Lighthouse Facts and Figures

• The first lighthouse at Barnegat was constructed in 1834, but the tower's small stature—a mere 40 feet, and an inferior light source, made it an inadequate aid to navigation for mariners. The structure stood until 1856, when it fell into the sea because of erosion.

• The present Barnegat Lighthouse was built in 1858 and was lit for the first time on January 1, 1859.

• The tower once showed a light from a first order Fresnel lens 165 feet above sea level. The lens was removed in 1927.

• Barnegat Lighthouse was discontinued on January 1, 1944.

• Today the first order Fresnel lens from Barnegat Lighthouse resides on display at the Barnegat Light Historical Museum.

• The State of New Jersey now owns Barnegat Lighthouse.

Photo by Ann-Marie Trapani

Liston Range Front Light
Delaware

Black Wave of Stench

Harry Spencer, Jr. loved life at Liston Range Front Light as a teenager in the 1930s. What kid wouldn't enjoy taking advantage of the carefree activities associated with living in a lighthouse by the water? From endless summertime swimming to adventurous walks along the marshes and sandy beach, Harry always found something to keep him content while his father, Harry, Sr., served as keeper of the light station from 1928 to 1943.

Liston Range Front Light is a beautiful, four-square, two-story structure situated on the Delaware River just above the point where the bay ends and the river begins at Liston's Point.

At 50-feet tall, the lighthouse sent a flashing white light 12 nautical miles down river to help guide vessels along the treacherous shipping channel of the Delaware. The panoramic view the lighthouse offered from atop the lantern room was breathtaking as well, but on one day in May of 1934, the word "breathtaking" would take on a whole new meaning—literally.

Beach Invasion

Keeper Spencer and his son Harry, Jr., wanted to get a good start to a fine sunny morning by heading outside to work in the yard. Harry set the scene saying, "Working outside that morning, dad and I periodically scanned the beach, which was somewhat norma,l when we noticed a long black line at the high tide mark. A most unusual sight to say the least."

Desiring to obtain a closer look at this mysterious sight, Keeper Spencer and his son jumped down over the concrete

seawall that safeguarded the light station property from the eva-
sive reach of the Delaware River's tidal surge and headed onto
the sandy beach. "Upon closer inspection, we discovered
mounds of Japanese Beetles," recalled Harry, Jr.

The beaching of the beetles was quite a first-time phenomenon at Liston Range Front Light. Never before had the Spencer
family seen anything like it. The line that snaked along water's
edge was no ordinary "mound" either. Harry described the

Photo by Bob Trapani, Jr.

Liston Range Front Light, south of Port Penn along the Delaware Bay

"black wave" of insects saying, "the mounds were at least one foot high and approximately two feet wide piled on the beach. Most of the beetles were still alive, and since the tide was at its highest point, the pile didn't move."

The cool refreshing tides soon took leave of the marooned black-shelled armada as the morning sun climbed to its zenith, parching what appeared to be millions of unsuspecting beetles. As the sand heated up with each passing hour, the rising temperatures punished and scorched many of the insects that quickly perished along the beach.

Harry remembered all too well the scene that followed—or smelled, to be exact—as the stench of death permeated the air, remarking, "When the sun came out fully, the stench was somewhat unbearable emitting from the decaying mounds of beetles."

Offensive Odor

The evening's incoming tides did little to carry away the awful odor or sickening sight. In fact, the Spencer's senses were tormented for the next couple of days. "It took three days of high tides and a stiff wind to dispense with them," said Harry. Yet the return of a golden-looking beach out in front of the lighthouse did not mean that the family was rid of the effects of the "black wave."

Many hundreds of thousands of beetles managed to escape the clutches of the sun's scorching rays by migrating to the surrounding areas of greens where they sought refuge from the heat.

Harry recalled that his father and mother were dismayed at this dilemma, saying, "Unfortunately, thousands found haven in the many flowers at the light station, particularly the rose bushes. It became almost epidemic."

Following the insect's invasion of their property, the U.S. Lighthouse Service made beetle traps available to the exasperated keeper. The traps were effective at capturing many numbers of the tormenting insects but they did little to reduce the nuisance to humans or the debilitating impact to greenery.

"You could easily catch a quart of beetles per day," said Spencer. "We actually burned the catch so that no other survived, hoping it would retard the population. It didn't."

In time, Mother Nature swept away the beetles as the seasons changed hands. But the memory of the summer of '34, when the "black wave" swept over the Liston Range Front Light Station, still burns bright in the mind of 85-year-old Harry Spencer, Jr.

Liston Range Front Light Facts and Figures

• The Liston Range was put into operation on October 25, 1904, but the historic lighthouse was not completed until December 1908. The front light for the range had been exhibited from a temporary wooden tower until the lighthouse was completed.

• The Liston Range Front Light was equipped with a fourth order Fresnel range lens that showed an occulting white light 50 feet above mean high water.

• The lighthouse was automated in 1948, and by 1953 it was decommissioned when the United States Coast Guard moved the light from the building to a modern skeletal tower that stood in the front yard of the light station.

• The lighthouse was sold at auction by the federal government to private owners in 1954.

• Today, the Liston Range Front Light is in beautiful condition and is listed in the National Register of Historic Places, thanks to the unwavering lighthouse preservation efforts of Dr. William Duncan.

Harry Spencer, Sr., keeper of the Liston Range Front Light, and his son, Harry, Jr., during the time the family lived at the lighthouse

Photo by Ann-Marie Trapani

Hereford Inlet Lighthouse
New Jersey

Bob Trapani, Jr.

Evading the Heavy Hand of Time

On the south side of Hereford Inlet, New Jersey, stands a beautiful Victorian Carpenter Gothic sentinel rising 57 feet in the air. When the elegant lighthouse was first lit in 1874 it sent out a fixed white light across the breakers to safeguard mariners entering both the inlet and transiting the Atlantic Ocean. Coastal craft sought the light's beam of light to guide them into the safe refuge of Hereford Inlet and away from turbulent storm seas, while ocean vessels utilized the lighthouse to lead them safely parallel to the Atlantic Ocean shoreline, south towards the entrance to Delaware Bay.

The wooden lighthouse was originally constructed safely away from the insatiable reaches of the Atlantic's raging surf within groves of cedar and holly trees. Yet despite the beacon's conservative placement along the sandy beach in the fishing village of Anglesea, Mother Nature was determined to methodically destroy the land protection of trees and plants in front of the structure—and ultimately the lighthouse itself if her erosion went unchecked.

Steve Murray, superintendent of Parks for the City of North Wildwood commented in his book, *A Guide to the Hereford Inlet Lighthouse Gardens*, that "The plant life in this 'plant community' just would not thrive too close to the ocean with the constant winds and salt spray." For some years after the sentinel's construction the native trees and plants that adorned the grounds around the light station flourished and even provided protection from erosion, "but that would change gradually over the next couple of decades," wrote Murray.

Battling Mother Nature

Inch by inch the ocean claimed ground in front of Hereford Inlet Lighthouse as ravaging currents swept valuable protective land out to sea. The great hurricane of October 1878 frightened lightkeeper Freeling H. Hewitt and his family so much that the keeper chose to abandon the lighthouse, thinking that its destruction was imminent as the storm's powerful seas lifted the structure off its block foundation.

Eleven years later in September 1889, a horrific storm of hurricane proportions held the lighthouse prisoner as seas encircled the beacon. Despite the harrowing conditions outside the lighthouse, keeper Hewitt maintained a vigilant watch and even saved the lives of 18 of his neighbors.

The storm surge was responsible for destroying, or severely damaging, nearby homes on the beach, forcing some of the Anglesea residents to seek shelter inside the lighthouse. Repairs were made to the ravaged beach at Hereford Inlet, but everyone knew that Mother Nature would come knocking again at some point in the future.

Over the years, the United States Lighthouse Service documented the ongoing impact of erosion at Hereford Inlet Lighthouse and stated in its 1897 Annual Report of the Light-House Board that, "The site, largely of loose, blowing sand," was being consumed at an alarming rate. The Service spent much in the way of money and effort to slow the effects of erosion by replacing fill and grading the light station property, but in the end, their efforts were in vain. Three years later, "flood waters and salt laden winds gnawed away at the plant life so that by 1900 the grounds were almost barren," according to Murray.

Mother Nature was both patient and relentless, as storm after storm inflicted irreversible damage to the property. Storm surge from winter nor'easters and the ebb and flow of the daily tides teamed up to encroach upon the helpless lighthouse. Spawning a ferocious summer tempest in August 1913, Mother Nature must have finally thought she was going to be successful in claiming Hereford Inlet Lighthouse for good. That year, destructive storm surge undermined the structure on the northeast side, causing it to list about 5 degrees.

In what amounted to be a huge wake-up call, the United States Lighthouse Service made hasty arrangements to move the unharmed sentinel back from the reaches of the ever-encroaching Atlantic Ocean. "A new location 150 feet west and along Central Avenue was chosen," said Murray. "The lot was cleared and graded and the lighthouse was moved to this spot by 1914."

Fighting Fires

Once the lighthouse was moved to safety, the preventative action might have thwarted Mother Nature but not Father Time. Storms may have been a major concern to the keepers of Hereford Inlet but an even greater day to day fear existed due to the building's wood construction—that of fire. At one point, during 1902, keeper Hewitt was terrified at the discovery of a fire in the ceiling over the kitchen. Without a moment to waste, Hewitt and his assistant worked frantically to extinguish the blaze before it spread to other defenseless parts of the lighthouse. Thanks to their quick action, the sentinel was saved from destruction.

Thirty-six years later, in 1938, Hereford Inlet Lighthouse again was threatened to become a blazing inferno.

The day started off like any other as keeper Ferdinand Heinzman attended to his duties around the light station. One of the projects he chose to work on was outside in the fresh air, applying a fresh coat of paint to the faded wood. Inside the building, his unsuspecting family was about to come face to face with the terror of fire.

The May 2, 1938, *Philadelphia Evening Bulletin* stated that the lightkeeper "was painting the exterior of the structure when the blaze broke out in a bedroom and spread to the nursery of his five year-old daughter, Shirley."

Ironically, the United States Lighthouse Service awarded Keeper Heinzman the Prestigious Efficiency Pennant for an impeccably kept light station just days before the fire. Given the obvious dedication to his occupation and the fact that his family was imminently threatened inside the lighthouse due to the developing blaze, one can imagine the tremendous anxiety he must have encountered the moment he realized the structure and his loved ones were in grave danger.

In his book *Northeast Lights*, author Robert G. Bachand described the pandemonium, saying, "Coast Guard personnel near the lighthouse were first to spot thick smoke coming from an upstairs bedroom." At this time, in addition to Shirley being in the nursery, Heinzman's wife, Anna, and another daughter were working in the kitchen as a stiff northeast breeze fanned the flames on the second floor, causing them to spread from the bedroom to the nearby nursery.

Bachand goes on to say, "A guardsman alerted the lighthouse and notified the local fire department. The keeper, hearing Anna call 'fire,' picked up an extinguisher and made his way to the bedroom, but heat and smoke drove him back. Grabbing a hose, he climbed a ladder and managed to douse the flames through an open window."

Keeper Heinzman's heroic efforts saved both the lighthouse and his family, but not before fire singed his hair as he attempted to enter the engulfed bedroom. The *Philadelphia Evening Bulletin* reported that a Coastguardsman also cut his hand while offering assistance and that several firemen were overcome by smoke. Following an investigation into what caused the fire, officials determined that the blaze originated in Anna's bedroom closet and was sparked by spontaneous combustion.

Photo by Ann-Marie Trapani

The rotating fourth order Fresnel lens that was once used at Hereford Inlet Lighthouse is now on display inside the museum.

Despite three major storms and two terrifying fires, Hereford Inlet Lighthouse continued to shine forth its lifesaving beam to sea over the years, safeguarding mariners and recreational boaters alike from the perils of the ocean.

Though the lighthouse was discontinued in 1964, sitting abandoned and endangered for 18 years, concerned citizens eventually stepped forward in 1982 to save the historic structure from succumbing to the indifferent hands of Father Time.

Over the following years, the community's efforts were successful in restoring the lighthouse and returning the light back up into the lantern room.

Today, while exhibiting the same unwavering dedication of Keeper Hewitt and courage of Keeper Heinzman, the passionate preservationists of the Hereford Lighthouse Commission proudly operate and maintain the lighthouse as a historic site and educational museum for the public.

Hereford Inlet Lighthouse Facts and Figures

• Hereford Inlet Lighthouse was completed on April 16, 1874, and was lit for the first time on May 11, 1874.

• The lighthouse stands 49.5 feet tall and shows a light to sea from a focal plane of 57 feet above sea level. The light's beam can be seen 13 nautical miles to sea.

• Hereford Inlet Lighthouse was active until 1964, when the U.S. Coast Guard took the light out of the historic building and erected a skeletal light tower out in front of the building. This tower was in service until 1986.

• The light was reestablished inside Hereford Inlet Lighthouse in 1986 and was subsequently relit as an aid to navigation. The light source is maintained by the United States Coast Guard Aids to Navigation Team, Cape May, New Jersey.

• The lighthouse is listed in the National Register of Historic Places.

• New Jersey Department of Environmental Protection leased the Hereford Inlet Lighthouse to the City of North Wildwood, and today the Hereford Lighthouse Commission impeccably maintains the historic site and beautiful gardens.

To learn more about the Hereford Inlet Lighthouse, visit the web site at www.herefordlighthouse.org

Hereford Inlet Lighthouse
1st & Central Ave.
North Wildwood, NJ 08260
Phone: (609) 522-4520

Photo by Ann-Marie Trapani

Fenwick Island Lighthouse
Delaware

Attack of the . . . Whales

O ne of the most dangerous portions of the Atlantic coast—between Cape Henlopen, Delaware, and Cape Henry, Virginia—for shipping interests in the 1800s and early 1900s. was found in the vicinity of Fenwick Island. The *1850 Blunt's American Coast Pilot* talks about this danger lurking off the southernmost coast of Delaware and northern portions of Maryland waters when it refers to the treacherous Fenwick Shoals, saying, "the coast is studded with shoals, lying at a distance of, from 3 to 6 miles from the nearest point of land."

These underwater hazards were so dangerous and caused so many shipwrecks that the United States Lighthouse Service eventually established the Fenwick Island Lighthouse in 1859 to help mariners avoid the shoals.

The presence of the 86-foot sentinel was no doubt a source of comfort to Captain Mitchell on a bright September day in 1895 as he piloted the steamer tug *Thomas J. Smith* near the vicinity of the dreaded Fenwick Shoals in route to Delaware Bay. The Fenwick Island Lighthouse's discernable daymark, which consists of a white tower and black lantern, could be seen rising above the Atlantic seascape, but on this day the coastal sentinel was powerless to help the captain with a danger beyond the influence of the shoals.

Unusual Development

The *Thomas J. Smith* was pulling a bone-laden Italian bark hailing from Buenos Aires to its port of call in Philadelphia when a nightmare scenario suddenly began to unfold before Captain

Mitchell's eyes. Without warning the tug and tow was attacked by a huge school of whales some 40 miles southeast of Cape Henlopen.

The *New Oxford Item*, a Pennsylvania newspaper, reported, "The whales surrounded the tug for a period of four hours, blowing large streams of water into the air, which completely shut out all view of the surroundings."

Visibility wasn't the only danger being posed to the frightened captain and crews of the tug and bark. The apparently angry whales were also creating a violent ruckus with the seas as each rise and plunge into the ocean tossed the craft perilously around as if it were caught in a sudden gale.

Captain Mitchell was mystified at his life threatening seaborne dilemma and was quoted as saying, "In thirty years' service at sea on tugs I never before saw such large whales, nor were they ever known to congregate in such numbers so close to land."

At the height of this seaborne terror the sailors must have thought they were doomed to go down to Davey Jones' Locker. The *New Oxford Item* went on to report, "It was a serious time on board the frail tug, and all hands were badly scared, as these monsters seemed infuriated and dashed along the sides of the boat with great force."

Facing imminent shipwreck from being swamped under the towering wakes caused by the whales or having their vessel broken in pieces by their ramming action, Captain Mitchell made a quick decision to try and outrun the school.

Ordering his engines to full speed, Captain Mitchell pushed ahead towards Delaware Bay, but no attempt to leave the whales behind was successful as the school kept violent pace with the tug and tow. Never more desperate, the captain resorted to reaching for a gun he kept with him on the boat.

"Finding that any attempt to get away from them was futile," said the news report, "Captain Mitchell loaded a large horse-pistol he had on board and began firing into them, but the bullets took no effect."

At one point, the terrified captain fired six shots at close range into the body of one of the whales, but his action not only failed to slow his adversary, it also served to further infuriate the mammal.

Following four hours of unspeakable danger, the terror-tossed tug and tow nearly gave up all hope of survival when suddenly the leader of the school headed offshore at 3 o'clock in the afternoon.

Minutes later the remainder of the whales followed suit and finally disappeared out of sight. The shaken crews of the tug and bark continued their journey up the bay and eventually arrived in Philadelphia to share their near-death experience on the high seas.

Fenwick Island Lighthouse Facts and Figures

- The lighthouse was finished construction in late 1858, but it was not lit for the first time until August 1, 1859.
- The Fenwick Island Lighthouse has a focal plane of 86 feet above sea level.
- When the light was first established its third order Fresnel lens showed a fixed white light, varied by one flash every two minutes. The light could be seen 15 nautical miles to sea under normal atmospheric conditions.
- From 1867 to 1881, two keepers and their families shared one house together until a second keeper's house was later constructed.
- The lighthouse was automated in the late 1940s or early 1950s, when electricity reached the light station.
- The United States Coast Guard decommissioned Fenwick Island Lighthouse as an active aid to navigation on December 13, 1978.
- The Friends of Fenwick Island Lighthouse were formed in 1981, the same year ownership of the lighthouse was transferred over to the state of Delaware.
- A symbolic light was displayed from atop the lighthouse on May 26, 1982.

To learn more about the efforts to preserve the Fenwick Island Lighthouse, contact:

Friends of the Fenwick Island Lighthouse
RR 3, Box 298
Fenwick Island, DE 19944

Elbow of Cross Ledge Lighthouse
New Jersey

Bob Trapani, Jr.

The Ledge of Doom

There is no lighthouse in the Delaware Bay with a more ominous history than Elbow of Cross Ledge. From the time it was built to its untimely demise, it was as if the dangerous Cross Ledge Shoal resisted the man-made sentinel's presence, and Neptune's rage remained stirred until destructive victory was ultimately in hand.

Though the U.S. Lighthouse Service in 1875 marked the southern portion of Cross Ledge Shoal, which runs parallel with the shipping channel on the eastern side with another light-house, an upper portion of the shoal was too close for comfort for ships traversing the bay.

This "elbow" is an awful hazard to vessels as the outcrop of the ledge lurks just a mere 400 to 500 feet eastward of the ship-ping channel. To make matters worse, this peril is situated on a critical turn—a turn many vessels never made before falling vic-tim to the ledge's unforgiving hold of death.

Maritime interests decided that the only way to protect ships from Cross Ledge was to build a lighthouse on the vicious shoal so a beam could pierce the night and warn mariners of the life-threatening dangers it presided over in the bay. The problem is some lighthouses seem simply not meant to be.

No Place for a Lighthouse

The first signs of forthcoming condemnation occurred while the U.S. Lighthouse Service made plans to root a caisson base deep within the bowels of Cross Ledge Shoal at the "elbow" in late 1907. While sinking the cast-iron caisson base 15 feet below the shoal, contractors encountered a series of frustrations and delays as dangerous currents, thrashing waves, quicksand at the site and even a collision between two barges seemed to give indication of the shoal's unrest. Even when the caisson was later completed atop the shoal, the base proved to be six inches out of level to the great dismay of the builders.

In his book, *Guiding Lights of the Delaware River and Bay*, lighthouse historian Jim Gowdy described the next mysterious dilemma to befall the builders of Elbow of Cross Ledge Lighthouse when he stated, "Then came a severe September storm, which caught the workmen and their floating equipment at the caisson." Gowdy went on to say, "Much of the working platform was washed away, and at least one workman was knocked overboard and drowned. In addition, one of the big work scows was torn loose by the waves, and sent adrift for two days, with only the government inspector in board. He was rescued in the vicinity of Maurice River Cove by one of the lighthouse tenders sent out to find him."

Three more years of commingled impediment and progress passed before the rugged beacon was finally completed and lit for the first time on February 1, 1910. The structure itself was described as a red brick, octagonal dwelling and situated on a brown cylindrical pier with a brown lantern. Mariners seeking to avoid the hazards of Cross Ledge Shoal could spot the beacon's white light some 13 nautical miles in the distance as it showed brightly 57 feet, 2 inches above Delaware Bay's mean high water. The lighthouse also was armed with a fog bell that could sound an audible warning should a shroud of fog or the gray murkiness of a tempest obscure its guiding light.

Once Elbow of Cross Ledge Lighthouse was officially placed on duty, countless ship captains blessed the beacon's presence each time they passed close by the deadly "elbow" of Cross Ledge Shoal on their way to ports of call.

However, the feeling of thankfulness was not shared by the light's keepers. In fact, men assigned to tend the flame of Elbow of Cross Ledge Lighthouse might have considered the duty equivalent to a death wish.

The December 19, 1954, issue of the *Philadelphia Evening Bulletin* described the keeper's fears, saying, "When visibility was poor, ships often passed so near the lighthouse that the whole building throbbed and shuddered from the vibration of the ship engines."

The account went on to say, "Ships had struck it glancing blows repeatedly, much to the concern of the men stationed there. It was no laughing matter that the four-man crew of the lighthouse slept in their lifejackets, ready to jump into the bay should their hazardous house come tumbling down."

Despite its many brushes with fate, Elbow of Cross Ledge Lighthouse served mariners for 41 years before King Neptune exacted his diabolical will on the men who kept the light burning bright.

In November 1951, a harrowing hurricane barreled up Delaware Bay, lashing out at the lighthouse at every turn. Though Elbow of Cross Ledge withstood the tempest's mighty punch, storm damage was so severe that the United States Coast Guard removed the sentinel's resident keepers thereafter.

Rather than enacting expensive repairs to the lighthouse to make it habitable again, the Coast Guard automated the beacon by running a submarine cable from Fortescue, New Jersey, out to the light in the bay. Another cable was run from Elbow of Cross Ledge south to Miah Maull Shoal Lighthouse, where the keepers at Miah Maull were tasked with "throwing the switch" each night to illuminate the lens atop the vacant sentinel.

Day of Destruction

Though Neptune had chased away the keepers of Elbow of Cross Ledge, he would not rest until the lighthouse was no more. After dodging near misses for many years, the fortunes of Elbow of Cross Ledge Lighthouse finally ran out on October 20, 1953. The day of reckoning threw a dense blanket of fog over Delaware Bay as the freighter *Steel Apprentice* groped its way along the shrouded shipping channel. Having passed Miah Maull Shoal Lighthouse in the middle of the bay, the ore-laden vessel charted its next turn along the perilous "elbow" of Cross Ledge Shoal to the north.

Both the captain and the pilot were standing side-by-side, outside on the wing of the ship's bridge trying in vain to see directly ahead of the bow. The anxiety of the moment was heightened by the fact that the ship's radar was inoperable and visibility was zero. In light of these less than desirable factors, the captain ordered the vessel to lower its speed and proceed with extreme caution up the channel. That's when the quiet of the moment was shattered by the cataclysmic din of crushing brick and screeching steel.

Appearing from out of nowhere was Elbow of Cross Ledge Lighthouse—or what was left of the stout sentinel. Despite its slow transiting speed, *Steel Apprentice* struck the lighthouse with such force that most of the superstructure was completely obliterated and sent overboard into a watery grave. When the captain and crew picked themselves off the deck of the ship, they observed the stark tragedy that left only the light's caisson base and about 10 feet of the shattered dwelling intact.

The captain was extremely distraught at the horrible thought that the lighthouse was manned and quickly asked the pilot whether there were keepers aboard the structure. Knowing no

Photo courtesy of the U.S. Coast Guard

Remains of the superstructure of Elbow of Cross Ledge Lighthouse, after being struck by the freighter Steel Apprentice.

one would have probably survived the horrific collision on the lighthouse, the captain was relieved to learn from the pilot that the beacon was automated only two years earlier. Though the caisson base remained on site, King Neptune finally achieved some measure of revenge on Elbow of Cross Ledge Lighthouse.

Following the disaster the U.S. Coast Guard erected the present-day red skeleton tower in 1954 and installed an automatic beacon atop the tower. During this time the color of the caisson was changed from brown to international orange for better visibility.

Today, shedder crabs cling to the base of the caisson just beneath the waterline chasing jellyfish as massive ships, some over 900-feet in length, continue to quietly pass by the light on their way to ports of call. Inside the structure's darkened caisson base the cracks, since repaired following the light's day of reckoning, still show through the concrete.

If you listen closely, the eerie quiet that reigns over Elbow of Cross Ledge Light will tell you a story—of a time when the sounds of silence were forever shattered by a sudden destructive impact of historical proportions.

Elbow of Cross Ledge Lighthouse Facts and Figures

• Elbow of Cross Ledge Lighthouse was completed and first lit on February 1, 1910
• The former lighthouse was described by the 1914 Light List for the Atlantic and Gulf Coasts, as a "red brick, octagonal dwelling, on brown cylindrical pier; brown lantern."
• Elbow of Cross Ledge Lighthouse once was equipped with a fourth order Fresnel lens that showed a white light 57' 2" above mean high water and could be seen up to 13 nautical miles.
• The lighthouse was automated in 1951 following damage from a hurricane that lashed Delaware Bay.
• The ore laden freighter *Steel Apprentice* slammed into the lighthouse during a dense fog on October 20, 1953. The violent collision destroyed the superstructure of the historic building.
• The U.S. Coast Guard established a modern skeletal tower atop the former light's caisson base in January 1955 and continues to maintain the light as an aid to navigation for ships transiting Delaware Bay.

Photo by Bob Trapani, Jr.

Mispillion Lighthouse
Delaware

Murder on the Bay

The 1873 Mispillion Lighthouse was beloved by the watermen on Delaware Bay, especially those working out of the local Slaughter and Cedar beaches. The beacon's white flashing light, 46 feet above sea level, was a friendly sight during times of intense darkness or stormy seas. But the glow exhibiting from atop Mispillion Lighthouse was indiscriminate, as it assisted and guided both the honorable activity of harvesting the bounty of the sea and the illegal bootlegging of liquor that occurred during Prohibition from 1920 to 1933.

Mispillion Lighthouse stood at the confluence of Cedar Creek and Mispillion River, the latter being the gateway to the City of Milford and its shipbuilding efforts some 10 miles up river. Though Milford was a thriving community, the area around the mouth of Mispillion River was desolate, with few residents to monitor or spot the illegal operations of local rumrunners. In fact, many such locations on both sides of Delaware Bay were perfect hideaways for bootleggers who violated the Prohibition Act of 1920 that outlawed making, transporting or selling liquor.

The Coast Guard Historian's web site talks about the rumrunner operations in the 1920s and 30s, saying, "The easiest way to get illegal liquor was to bring it from outside the country. Ships loaded with liquor waited offshore, outside U.S. waters, for small speedboats that ferried the contraband ashore in the dark of night."

This practice made out-of-the-way locations like Mispillion River a perfect backdrop to operate from—one that law enforcement authorities could not easily police.

Though the rumrunners were routinely engaged with avoiding or, in some cases, battling the U.S. Coast Guard and their fleet of cutters, the bootleggers also could turn on their own in the same violent manner that made them notoriously feared by law biding citizens. One such case occurred under the guiding beam of Mispillion Lighthouse in June 1930. Anytime illegal activities prove to be a lucrative endeavor by those who undertake the risks of breaking the law, murder is often a despicable tool in the never ending power play.

Attacked by Pirates

The June 24, 1930, edition of the *Lima News* of Ohio caught the eye of its morning readers with a ghastly headline and accompanying story that started off stating, "Six members of the crew of a mystery yacht are believed to have met death at the hands of Delaware Bay freebooters following the discovery of the battered hulk of the yacht drifting idly with the tides in Delaware Bay today."

The motive of the attack was unknown, as was the identity of the bloody-handed assailants who committed the atrocities. Was it revenge or jealousy by a fellow bootlegger, or did a few locals decide that raiding the vessel laden with illegal spirits was too alluring to pass up? No one seems to know, or at least no one was openly saying. But investigating authorities surmised that the vessel and crew were overtaken by a pirate craft and looted.

Regardless, the act of murder was not the only vicious act demonstrated at the scene, as the yacht itself was treated harshly by the attackers, who tore open a huge hole in the side of the boat in an effort to remove the liquor. The *Lima News* account stated that, "Without a clue as to the whereabouts of the crew, authorities today were of the belief that they had been brutally murdered and their bodies cast into the bay."

The U.S. Coast Guard out of Cape May, New Jersey, secured the crime scene and eventually removed approximately $10,000 of liquor. It was unknown how much of the cargo of spirits was removed from the starboard side of the yacht, but Coastguardsmen were able to determine that a great struggle of death occurred in the hold of the vessel. The ill-fated crew's clothing and other personal effects were found strewn about the floor, which indicated to the Coast Guard the number of personnel operating the boat at the time of the attack.

The doomed yacht was identified as the *Daisy T*, a 45-foot speedster that became partially submerged in Delaware Bay following the deadly looting. When found by the Coast Guard to be abandoned and adrift, the boat was a few miles below the mouth of the Mispillion River—a place noted by the *Lima News* as "a haven for rumrunners."

No doubt the perpetrators utilized the guiding light shining forth from Mispillion Lighthouse to help them bring their ill-gotten gain ashore and escape the hand of justice. As for the Mispillion Lighthouse, its days as a beacon for navigation were numbered. By 1929, the United States Lighthouse Service decided to decommission the wooden sentinel and move its duties to an automated skeletal tower adjacent to the lighthouse—four years before Prohibition itself would be relegated to the pages of history.

Mispillion Lighthouse Facts and Figures

• At least three lighthouses stood on the banks of the Mispillion River, with previous structures being built in 1831 and 1839—prior to the 1873 lighthouse being constructed.
• The 1873 sentinel was originally painted in a gray or buff color and a black lantern—a contrast to the red color that Mispillion Lighthouse become known for in later years.
• The lighthouse once possessed a 6th order Fresnel lens, the smallest or least powerful order of lenses. This was due to the fact that the river was not considered of great navigational importance to the United States Lighthouse Service since local watermen were generally the only traffic that utilized the beacon.
• The Mispillion Lighthouse was automated in 1929 and sold to private owners in 1932.
• A group of concerned citizens from in and around the Slaughter Beach area formed the Keepers of the Mispillion Light during 2001, in an effort to save the historic lighthouse from being lost to neglect and time.
• A tragic lightning strike destroyed much of the historic lantern room and caused fire damage throughout the historic lighthouse on May 2, 2002.
• The remaining portions of the structure were sold to and moved from the light station site in June 2002, and are presently (2005) being incorporated into a replica of the Mispillion Lighthouse that will stand in Shipcarpenter Square, Lewes, Delaware.

Photo by Bob Trapani, Jr.

Ship John Shoal Lighthouse
New Jersey

Shoal of Unrest

S hip John Shoal, located at the head of Delaware Bay, has historically been both a dangerous position for navigation and an area of great mystery and intrigue. Though Colonial America was keenly aware of the underwater hazards that lurked at this part of the bay, there was little means available to mark and warn mariners of its deadly presence.

Throughout the late 1700s, pilots with expert local knowledge knew enough to avoid this perilous shoal whenever possible, but no one identified the danger by name— that was until one fateful Christmas Eve near the turn of the century.

On December 24, 1797, Captain Robert Folger pushed forward up the ice-laden Delaware River—despite the menacing presence of innumerable frozen masses floating aimlessly downriver—with hopes of making his port of call in Philadelphia by Christmas morning. Captain Folger's journey up the bay, with his ship *John* and 50 or more German passengers, seemed to be going well enough, until he reached an area referred to as the Middle Grounds in the Delaware Bay, opposite Cohansey River, New Jersey.

Wreck of the 'John'

Whether Captain Folger was unfamiliar with the safe limits of the shipping channel or his ship was carried off course against its will by the influence of ice floes is not known. But the end result of being shipwrecked was the same for the *John*.

Without a moment's notice, the unsuspecting vessel was caught in the unforgiving clutches of a hard sandy shoal. The ship's forward momentum—unimpeded by any thought of danger, ensured the shoal gained a deep grasp that would make escape impossible. Despite the ship's dire state, the passengers and crew were able to safely abandon the *John* and seek safe refuge at the village of Greenwich, along the Cohansey River.

The Captain, his crew and some locals went back to the ship to salvage the valuable cargo—of cordage, linen, Swedish iron, Russian sheeting, sailcloth, copper sheets and nails, window glass, hollow glass and German toys. Though much of the ship's goods were saved, the same could not be said for the vessel itself. Passing ice floes had cut deeply into its hull and eventually sliced the doomed vessel to pieces. The underwater sandbank that claimed the *John* would thereafter be known as Ship John Shoal.

The horrific dangers caused by Ship John Shoal to shipping persisted until 1872, when Congress tried to counter the shoal's deadly presence by approving a lighthouse to be built at the site. Apparently, the danger posed by Ship John Shoal to sailing vessels wasn't limited to ships actually having to ground on the hazard. The shoal could even "lure" unsuspecting mariners to their doom by the subtle use of the irresistible tides.

The *1872 Annual Report of the Light-House Board* attests to this diabolical threat, stating, "The necessity for a light on Ship John Shoal is to guide vessels up the channel and prevent them from getting ashore on Ship John Shoal and the one opposite, the tide being such as to drift them at times on either shoal. This drifting is frequently experienced in this part of the channel."

By 1875, contractors commenced work at the site and established a caisson lighthouse base deep within the bowels of the treacherous sandbank. Showing continued unrest since the wreck of *John* back in 1797, it was as if the shoal was going to resist any attempt to subdue its powers of death and destruction right from the outset. After citing great difficulties with sinking the caisson at Ship John Shoal, the *1875 Annual Report of the Light-House Board* went on to state how "Old Man Winter" and the sinister shoal teamed up to wreak havoc on the contractors building the lighthouse.

The report stated that "The past winter was one of great severity, and the structure was probably subjected to as severe a test as it will be ever again." After this presumptuous statement, the report went on to recount the dangers encountered by the keepers who were tending the temporary light atop the incomplete caisson. Evidently the lightkeepers feared that the power of the ice would cause the shoal to release the base from its grasp and subsequently send them to a watery grave.

Though the report stated that the caisson came through the harrowing period unharmed, "The keepers, however, became alarmed for their personal safety, and abandoned their posts on the 18th of January, 1875. Owing to the quantity of ice in the Delaware, it was impossible to reach the work again until the 13th of March, when it was found unharmed, and the light was re-exhibited."

The unrest of Ship John Shoal continued into the following year as changing currents altered the physical makeup of the sandbank, deepening the area around the caisson lighthouse and washing away much of its protective rip-rap that was placed at the foundation to guard against ice floes. Eventually, the light-house was completed and first lit on August 10, 1877, despite Mother Nature's strong resistance.

Even though a lighthouse was now standing guard over Ship John Shoal, the underwater hazard remained a wary dread for mariners and watermen alike, especially during periods of thick fog.

The shoal's influence on waterborne shipping was renowned, but was it possible for disaster to occur simply by fly-ing over top of it?

Up, Up and Away

The answer to that question appears to be an easy "No." But a hot air balloon "shipwreck" at Ship John Shoal on May 9, 1911, sure added a mysterious twist to the sandbank's storied legend.

The hot air balloon *Philadelphia II* slipped the surly bonds of earth at 9:30 a.m., rising high above the Earth for a leisurely day amongst the clouds. The balloon's owner, Thomas E. Eldridge, owner and president of the Philadelphia Aeronautical Recreation Society, was joined by two distinguished friends—Ada Turner Kurtz, celebrated vocalist, and John H. Noggle, president of the Pennsylvania Chemical Company.

The trio's fun in the sun was going as planned until the first signs of trouble occurred at 1 o'clock in the afternoon. The *Philadelphia II* was suddenly being blown out over the Delaware River and down the bay by fickle winds, and no amount of effort by Mr. Eldridge to steer the aircraft made a positive difference.

At this point the crew became extremely alarmed, and fearing that they would be escorted against their will on the wings of the wind out into the Atlantic Ocean, the trio screamed for help to a passing tug below on the bay at Ship John Shoal Lighthouse. The would-be heroes on the tug *Mary J. Walker* grabbed lines being dropped from the hot air balloon at a height of 285 feet and made them fast to their bobbing vessel. Once the lines were secured, the opposite direction resistance of the tug and balloon caused the *Philadelphia II* to swoop down over the bay and zigzag uncontrollably behind the *Mary J. Walker.*

The May 10, 1911, edition of the *Washington Post* described the terror that followed, saying, "The occupants were nearly thrown from the basket several times. Practically all the ballast was cast overboard, the ropes swung over the side, and finally cut loose and the anchor cast away. Everything was done to keep the balloon above water until the arrival at Delaware City."

Despite making all possible attempts to lighten the basket's weight, the balloon was immersed twice in Delaware Bay at Ship John Shoal Lighthouse before taking "flight" again thanks to the tug pulling hard up the channel. At one point, the balloon's crew was so desperate to keep the basket airborne that Mr. Noggle risked his life by sliding down the line to the tugboat below to decrease the weight of the *Philadelphia II.* The badly shaken balloonists were finally delivered to safety at a landing in Delaware City—their basket only a few feet above the wharf.

Frightening winds swirling in the bay at Ship John Shoal Light may not have claimed the passengers of the hot air balloon as victims of its treachery, but the shoal's hideous reputation won out during a future tragedy that took place in the shadow of the sentinel.

The *Lima Times Democrat* newspaper in Ohio reported on March 7, 1913, that a sudden gale caught three workmen by surprise and all alone on Delaware Bay. Prior to the storm's arrival, contractors were working at Ship John Shoal Lighthouse to raise a sunken barge that was previously claimed by the legendary sandbank. After toiling at their task for a good part of the day, the tug decided to go ashore for unexplained reasons, leaving the pile driver with its three-man crew at the site.

Shortly after the tug's departure, 70-mile-per-hour winds from a rising gale suddenly swept over the open waters of the bay, placing the workmen in grave danger. The waves quickly grew in height and ferociousness as the pile driver started to dip and tilt side to side. The developing chaos gave the impression that the enraged shoal was not about to relinquish the sunken barge, nor allow the crew working to raise the immersed craft to escape with their own lives at the same time.

Without warning the pile driver capsized in the frothy water, enabling Ship John Shoal to add another "prize" to its long list of unfortunate wrecks. The newspaper account stated, "When the pile driver sank it took a yawl with it, removing the only means of escape for the workmen." The three-person work crew was never found, and it was presumed that they had drowned in the turbulent waters of the bay.

Ship John Shoal Lighthouse Facts

•   Ship John Shoal Lighthouse exhibited a light for the first time on August 10, 1877.
•   The lighthouse once showed a fixed white light from a fourth order Fresnel lens 53 feet above high water. Today, the lighthouse is equipped with a modern Vega VRB-25 optic and is maintained by the United States Coast Guard Aids to Navigation Team, Cape May, New Jersey.
•   When first built, the lighthouse color scheme consisted of black caisson base, brown dwelling and black lantern room. Today, the lighthouse is painted red.
•   Ship John Shoal Lighthouse was automated in 1973.
•   The lighthouse's fourth order Fresnel lens is now on display at the United States Coast Guard Group Air Station, Atlantic City, New Jersey.

Brandywine Shoal Lighthouse
New Jersey

Vanished Without a Trace

F ew locations in the expansive Delaware Bay were more
dangerous to mariners than Brandywine Shoal. The nearly
three-mile-long underwater obstruction lurks just beneath
the surface of the bay at varying depths of 1 to 17 feet on the
eastern side of the main shipping channel at the southern part of
Delaware Bay.

To safeguard commercial shipping and watermen from the
deadly grasp of the shoal, the federal government erected
America's first screwpile lighthouse on the lower end of the hazard in 1850.

A Functional Light

What the iron lighthouse lacked in beauty, it more than
made up for in terms of navigational value. A seafaring captain
by the name of Robert Bosworth penned a letter to the Secretary
of the Treasury in 1852, praising the new lighthouse, saying, "I
would take occasion here to say, that the beacon light lately put
up on Brandywine Shoal, is the most brilliant of anything that I
have seen on our coast."

Other mariners strongly supported Captain Bosworth's claim
by indicating that the light at Brandywine Shoal—the first
encountered after passing the Delaware capes, could be seen
more easily on the approach to Delaware Bay than its much
taller counterparts at Cape Henlopen and Cape May.

The reason for the light's brilliance was due to a third order
lens that resided in the lantern, which sent a piercing white
beam 13.5 nautical miles over the seascape to alert ships of the
deadly danger it stood sentinel over. In addition, the light station
was armed with a mighty fog bell that sounded an ominous

warning to steer clear in times when thick fog shrouded the nearby waters of the bay. Yet even with a dazzling light and a deafening audible warning from the fog bell, vessels still foundered on the treacherous Brandywine Shoal.

On July 7, 1905, the *Elyria Reporter* newspaper from Ohio carried a story of intrigue and demise surrounding a yacht's fatal encounter with the death-dealing shoal. A few days prior to the tragic incident, two other yachts—the *Zealand* and *Circe* accompanied the ill-fated yacht *Markette*, as they departed the Corinthian Yacht Club's anchorage in Philadelphia for a cruise down the bay. The newspaper account reported that late that Saturday afternoon, a storm swept over Delaware Bay and grounded the *Markette* hard fast on the shoal near the Brandywine Shoal Lighthouse.

The *Markette*, which was owned by Dr. Hubert A. Hare, a prominent Philadelphia physician, immediately hailed the yacht *Circe* for assistance as seas began to pound against the stricken vessel. The *Circe* was able to get close enough to safely remove Doctor Hare and his friend, Lucius S. Landreth, and take them to safety in Lewes, Delaware. The *Elyria Reporter* stated that, "The crew of four men were left aboard to care for the vessel with the understanding that a tug would at once be sent to pull the yacht off the shoal."

Fruitless Rescue

True to his word, Doctor Hare did indeed contact help as soon as he reached shore. The tug Juno was informed of the yacht's dilemma at Delaware Breakwater and immediately steamed toward Brandywine Shoal, over 10 miles up Delaware Bay. In the meantime, the storm continued to blow unabated over the open waters, sending water in and over the shipwrecked yacht. Realizing their situation was becoming quite dire, the four crewmen knew that few options existed when it came to escaping what was sure to be a watery grave if they did not soon abandon ship.

To the dismay of the would-be rescuers, the crew of the Juno discovered that the *Markette* had sunk in the shipping channel by the time they arrived on the scene. Scanning the storm-tossed waters, the *Juno* was unable to locate the four crewmen. Doctor Hare was distraught over the fact that the men were missing and immediately hired several launches in the area to patrol Delaware Bay and along the coastline in hopes of finding his crew alive.

The newspaper account reported the grim tidings that the hope of finding the men alive was all but gone, saying, "Last evening Fred Vogel who had been searching with the launch *Hilda* in the vicinity of the wreck, returned with the *Markette's* launch." The newspaper went on to state, "He reported that he had found the launch, bottom up, near the Brandywine Lighthouse. The keeper of the lighthouse informed him that the last he saw of the crew was shortly before dark Saturday evening when they were in the launch trying to make the Delaware shore. It is believed the launch was upset in the rough sea that was running and that the four men were drowned."

Brandywine Shoal Lighthouse Facts and Figures

• From *The Modern Lighthouse Service* by Arnold Burges Johnson in 1890...Brandywine Shoal Lighthouse, in Delaware Bay, about 8 miles from the ocean, was begun in 1848 and lighted in 1850, costing $53,317 for the lighthouse, and $11,485 for the surrounding ice-breaker. This was the first lighthouse built in the United States on Mitchell's screwpile, which takes its name from the inventor of its broad helicoidal flange, an auger pod, which, by merely turning, is bored into sand, mud, or other penetrable bottom, so as to form a foundation with a broad bearing, on which the weight of a columnar structure may be safely diffused, and to which it is firmly fastened.

• The 1850 lighthouse showed a fixed white light 46-feet above sea level. The iron superstructure was painted red in color with green shutters.

• A new Brandywine Shoal Lighthouse was completed in 1914 to take the place of the outdated 1850 sentinel. The new beacon was built adjacent to the old structure.

• The 1914 conical lighthouse stands 60 feet tall and is constructed of concrete. The entire structure is painted white, with a red lantern room.

• Brandywine Shoal Lighthouse has the distinction of being the last Delaware Bay lighthouse to have resident keepers before their presence was removed in 1974.

• Brandywine Shoal Lighthouse remains an active aid to navigation and is maintained by U.S. Coast Guard Aids to Navigation Team, Cape May, New Jersey.

Cape Henlopen Lighthouse
Delaware

Bob Trapani, Jr.

Act of War Darkens 'Old Man of the Sea'

The legendary Cape Henlopen Lighthouse observed a wealth of American history unfold below its stately perch atop the "Great Sand Dune" of Cape Henlopen, Delaware. Built in 1765, the "Old Man of the Sea" enjoyed a front row seat to many of our nation's most historic events, including the Revolutionary War, an eight-year struggle that would finally give birth to a nation.

In all, the venerable beacon rendered 159 years of faithful service and established a world renowned reputation as being a friend to seafarers of all nationalities. A supplement to the *1902 Delaware Pilot* attests to this fact, stating, "To a sea-tossed mariner there is no more welcome sight than the fixed white light that surmounts the tower of Henlopen, itself almost ghost-like in its whiteness."

Resisting the British

After only 12 years of duty, the "Old Man of the Sea" went dark during the early years of the patriots' battle for freedom. And it would remain so for the duration of the Revolutionary War.

Legend has it that during the second week of April, 1777, a British man-of-war, the *Roebuck*, and a sloop-of-war, both which were known to be operating in Delaware waters, dropped anchor one night under the icy stare of the steady white beam emitting from Cape Henlopen Lighthouse. The intention of the two ships was to send a landing party to the cape in order to obtain quantities of beef for His Majesty's frigates at anchor off the Delaware capes.

A longboat with a squadron of British soldiers was subsequently launched and rowed toward the lighthouse—eventually pulling their boat through the breakers and onto the beach. After an arduous walk through the soft, wind blown sand of the cape, the military men arrived at the foot of the sentinel prepared to deliver their demands to the keeper.

After hearing that the troops wanted to remove a few of the cattle that were grazing on the cape, the old lightkeeper identified by a newspaper account as Hedgecock, proved anything but cooperative. Even his mannerisms were evidently nonchalant and smug as the keeper was described as "smoking his pipe in the doorway of his eight-sided tower," just before delivering his verbal blow to the man in charge of the envoy.

According to the March 21, 1926, article by Thomas Hill of the *New York Times*, Hedgecock reportedly said, "I'll give you no cows, but if you don't get out I'll give you some bullets!" Such a defiant reply was sure to bring consequences as the British contingent made an about face and returned to their ships to deliver the keeper's terse reply to their commanding officer.

Keeper Hedgecock believed the lighthouse to be safe from harm's way, as the cannons on the *Roebuck* would more than likely be unable to reach the structure from its distance in the water. He felt, even if the guns of the warship managed to travel the distance between them, the walls of the lighthouse being six feet thick would prove to be more than adequate protection against enemy fire.

The commander of the *Roebuck* was also aware of the fact that firing a few retaliatory volleys toward the lighthouse was a wasted effort. Instead, the order was issued to send several longboats ashore to procure by force what Keeper Hedgecock refused to relinquish peacefully. In the meantime, the lightkeeper maintained a careful watch over the activity around the ships and became quite alarmed when he noticed a number of longboats carrying soldiers rowing back to the cape with a purpose obviously in mind.

The *New York Times* article captured the chaotic scene at this moment, saying, "A landing party surprised the keeper and his assistants instead of the expected bombardment. It was well for the keepers that fully a mile separated the lighthouse from the sea in those days."

The keepers made haste and gathered up everything of value before running for safe cover within the thick groves of pine trees behind the Cape Henlopen Lighthouse. In the process of vacating the light station, the keepers attempted to also drive as many cattle before them as possible.

In the meantime, the British soldiers slowly advanced toward the lighthouse—their march proving quite cumbersome in the shifting sands of the cape. Exhausted from their sandy tramp, the squadrons of men saw their anger and frustrations boil over at discovering the timely retreat of the keepers and their cattle.

According to Thomas Hill's account, "The British, finding nothing else at hand to confront the landing party, took out their spite on the lighthouse. They set its interior woodwork and wooden stairs merrily ablaze. Down from the top hurtled the oil hand-lamp, which was the Henlopen Light of that period, together with the circular table upon which it rested, and its tiny reflectors."

Knowing that the light's impenetrable six-foot walls could not be damaged, the vengeful-minded soldiers turned their attention to other facets of the light station property—after being satisfied with terrorizing the interior of the sentinel. The other objects of their rage included the keeper's house and nearby oil shed, both which were purportedly burned as well. Finally, the British contingent followed the tracks of the cattle into the pine

Photo courtesy of the U.S. Coast Guard

The Cape Henlopen Lighthouse, towering over the Atlantic Ocean, toppled to its destruction from atop the Great Dune on April 13, 1926.

forest, where they were able to round up a few stray stragglers before heading back to the *Roebuck*.

The result of the act of war inflicted upon Cape Henlopen Lighthouse would scar the beacon for the remainder of the Revolutionary War. Rather than being able to send out its guiding beam from atop the golden sands of the cape to sea, the light-house remained a hollow structure, with its charred interior a constant reminder of that fateful encounter. It was not until 1783 that the Board of Wardens of the Port of Philadelphia was able to enact critical repairs to the structures at the light station. By 1784, Cape Henlopen Lighthouse was shining bright once more—going dark again for a brief time during the War of 1812 and finally for good in 1924.

Historical Perspective

Some historians though have questions about the story of the *Roebuck's* aggression at Cape Henlopen Light Station, and some are interesting arguments that create quite a mystery.

Though the actual logs of the man-of-war confirm the fact that the ship was indeed around Cape Henlopen in April, May and June of 1777, there is no mention of any landing on the cape or at the lighthouse.

According to lighthouse historian John W. Beach, "It is unlikely that they (the British) would burn the same light that helped guide them in and out of the Delaware Bay, or fail to record the event in the ship's log if they did burn it." Beach goes on to say, "It is a matter of record that the interior of the light-house was burned, but a matter for dispute as to when it occurred and who did the burning. Could the lighthouse keeper have become careless while filling his oil lamp and set his own lighthouse on fire, or did the British, in fact, land and set the structure afire?"

The answer to this intriguing mystery will never be known. This secret and all of the venerable sentinel's illustrious history went to a watery grave when Cape Henlopen Lighthouse toppled to its destruction from atop the Great Dune on April 13, 1926.

Cape Henlopen Lighthouse Facts and Figures

• Cape Henlopen Lighthouse was built in 1765 and was the sixth beacon constructed in colonial America
• Following the formation of the Federal government in the wake of the Revolutionary War, the Commonwealth of Pennsylvania deeded the title to the light station to the United States on September 28, 1789. It is interesting to note that though Cape Henlopen Lighthouse stood on Delaware soil, it was actually Philadelphia maritime interests in Pennsylvania that paid for the construction and operation of the beacon—thus owning the lighthouse from afar.
• During the 161 years the lighthouse stood, the point was extended over 3,700 feet at an average of around 23 feet per year.
• An 1851 inspection of the light station listed Cape Henlopen Lighthouse as being 84 feet from its base to the top of the structure's lantern, and the lighthouse exhibited a light 164 feet above the tides—the focal plane from sea. The report also stated that the lighthouse was built of ashlar granite or gneiss, with an interior of rubble masonry.
• The lighthouse received a beautiful and powerful first order Fresnel lens for the first time on December 12, 1855.
• Due to ceaseless erosion and undermining of the structure's foundation, the Cape Henlopen Lighthouse was decommissioned on October 1, 1924.
• The light's first order Fresnel lens was removed and placed in storage at the Edgemoor Lighthouse Depot. A tragic fire destroyed that building and lens on April 28, 1925.
• The final chapter for Cape Henlopen Lighthouse came on April 13, 1926, when the sentinel fell from atop the Great Dune and into the sea on a bright sunny day.

Photo courtesy of the U.S. Coast Guard

Cape Henlopen Beacon Light
Delaware

Bob Trapani, Jr.

Keeper and His Family Rescued from Perils of the Sea

L ighthouses were built to save lives and cargo by piercing the realm of nightfall with a guiding beam, which pointed mariners the way to safe port. The lightkeeper and his family were responsible for ensuring the light was sent out to sea each night, and thus played a direct role in helping to save countless numbers of lives along America's coastal waterways over the past three centuries.

But on rare occasions Mother Nature's wrath would even place the keepers of the light in precarious situations beyond their control. One such dilemma occurred at the Cape Henlopen Beacon Light Station in 1884.

The beacon light worked with the legendary Cape Henlopen Lighthouse to help guide ships past the dangerous and ever extending sandy tip of the cape. But just like the earlier 1825 Cape Henlopen Beacon, which was undermined by ravaging waves sweeping across the cape region, the 1864 screw-pile structure was soon similarly assaulted, despite its construction design that was better suited to handle the effects of the over reaching Atlantic Ocean.

Steady Assault by the Sea

During the ensuing years, the beacon's lightkeeper watched as the Atlantic Ocean slowly encroached on the light station. High tides were reaching under the screw-pile structure by 1883, methodically eroding away the sandy foundation that supported

85

the lighthouse. The *1884 Annual Report of the Lighthouse Board* foretold the doom of the Cape Henlopen Beacon Light, reporting: ". . . the beach is being cut away under this station, so that at nearly every high tide, the sea comes under the house. In December 1883, brush loaded with stone was placed around the station, which caused the sand to bank up but in a few weeks, a storm carried it all away. The station is in good order but cannot be considered safe, as a single long violent storm might throw down the beacon."

On the night of January 9, 1884, the serious concerns over the pending doom of the light station almost became prophetic as the lifesaving power of the Cape Henlopen Beacon Light was nearly extinguished by a high running, wind-driven surf. In fact, the irony of this harrowing night was that it would turn out that Lighthouse Keeper Joseph Hall and his family would be the ones who needed to be saved from the perils of the sea.

A strong southeast wind was blowing and a heavy sea running on the morning of January 9th when Surfman Maull left the Cape Henlopen Life-Saving Station for the midnight to 4 a.m. patrol.

Trudging northward through thick sand and avoiding the breakers pounding the Cape, Surfman Maull eventually came upon the imperiled light keeper and his family, who were trapped atop the screw-pile structure. At that point, the

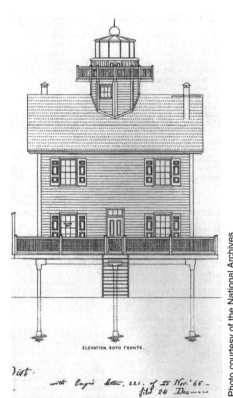

ELEVATION BOTH FRONTS.

list.

with Engr letter, 221, of 25 Nov '65 –
filed 24 Dec –

An architect's elevation sketch of the light above the keeper's home (1864-1884)

Photo courtesy of the National Archives

strong seas had washed away the exterior staircases and were threatening to bring down the lighthouse altogether. Keeper Hall hailed the assistance of Surfman Maull, but the lifesaver was powerless to rescue the light keeper and his family without help and equipment.

Meanwhile, at the lifesaving station, Keeper John A. Clampitt began to worry when his No. 3 surfman didn't return at 4 a.m., especially since the seas were heavy and a thick fog was prevailing at the same time. Keeper Clampitt quickly acted on the situation by dispatching another surfman to search for the missing crew member.

"Patrol No. 2 left the station 4 o'clock, had great difficulty in getting to the point of cape as the sea was cutting slews through the beach," Keeper Clampitt recorded in his daily station log. "When he (Surfman Howard) got to the point of the cape, he met patrol No. 3 working his way back to the station for assistance to get the people out of the lighthouse as they were in danger of the house being washed down. . . their escape having washed away and heavy pieces of wreckage washing up against the piling."

Rescue by the Crew

Once Surfman Maull returned to the lifesaving station, he explained the danger to the light keeper and his family. The news prompted Keeper Clampitt to hastily summon and brief his crew of the situation before springing into action.

Keeper Clampitt later penned this description of the rescue in his daily station log, saying, "As soon as I got the news, I started with five men to assist them in getting ashore. As soon as we got to the lighthouse, I found the tide had run off so we could wade to the house and with the aid of a 16-foot ladder, we got on the porch. I went in the house, found the people very much excited and wanted to land. I told the keeper to get the lady and child ready and we would land them, which we did in very few moments. We took the woman and child to the big lighthouse and the keeper went to the fog horn to relieve the keeper who was on watch at the fog horn at the time. We all arrived back to the station about 11 o'clock."

It is worth noting that not only did the surfmen of the United States Life-Saving Service perform their duties admirably, by rescuing the keeper and his family from the endangered lighthouse but that Keeper Hall himself exhibited an incredible sense of duty as well.

Despite being trapped by raging seas during a sleepless night and enduring great stress and anxiety for the safety of his wife and child, Keeper Joseph Hall did not beg off the duty of relieving his counterpart at the Cape Henlopen Fog Signal Station. This selfless sense of duty was a tribute to both Keeper Hall and the United States Lighthouse Service.

As for the Cape Henlopen Beacon, the end was near. The *1885 Annual Report* records the light's demise, stating: "This beacon, having become unsafe from the undermining of its screw pile foundation, the light was, on October 1, 1884, discontinued and the beacon, with the exception of the piles, was removed."

The United States Lighthouse Service established the Delaware Breakwater East End Lighthouse in 1885 to assume the duties of the doomed beacon light of guiding mariners around the dangerous cape. The ever-shifting sands that undermined the Cape Henlopen Beacon would also later claim the legendary Cape Henlopen Lighthouse, when the stately sentinel toppled from the "Great Dune" into the surf below on April 13, 1926.

The second Cape Henlopen Beacon, built in 1825

Photo courtesy of the U.S. Coast Guard

Cape Henlopen Beacon Facts and Figures

• According to lighthouse historian Jim Gowdy, "The Cape Henlopen Beacon was established because the sandy point of land upon which the Cape Henlopen Lighthouse was built 1765, continued to grow northward beyond the lighthouse. By 1824, the lighthouse was about one mile south of the point of Cape Henlopen. The expanding tip of the cape was a danger to shipping, and the Cape Henlopen Beacon was built in 1825."

• The first Cape Henlopen Beacon did not have a keeper on site. The keeper from the Cape Henlopen Lighthouse was asked to tend both lights by making a two-mile round trip multiple times a day—and in all kinds of weather, to ensure both lights were burning bright.

• By 1854 the United States Lighthouse Service outfitted the beacon light with a fourth order Fresnel lens and finally built a keeper's quarters on site for separate men to tend this lighthouse, rather than the crew at Cape Henlopen Lighthouse.

• Over the years, the cape continued to extend northwestward, necessitating the construction of a new Cape Henlopen Beacon Lighthouse. The old structure was torn down and a new screw-pile lighthouse was completed on December 20, 1864.

• The lighthouse showed a fixed white light from a fourth order Fresnel lens 45 feet above sea level. The light could be seen 12 nautical miles out over the Atlantic Ocean.

• The light station received a first order steam fog signal on September 15, 1875.

• Severe undermining of the lighthouse caused the United States Lighthouse Service to discontinue the Cape Henlopen Beacon on October 1, 1884.

Cross Ledge Lighthouse
New Jersey

Bob Trapani, Jr.

Target Practice and Fire

F ew lighthouses have ever suffered a more humiliating experience in a long but final dance into oblivion.

Becoming obsolete, Cross Ledge Lighthouse absorbed the ill effects of abandonment, vandalism, the indignity of being utilized for target practice, and finally, fell victim to the all-consuming power of the flame.

Lighthouse historian Jim Gowdy summed up the sad dilemma of the beacon at Cross Ledge Shoal, saying, "The Cross Ledge Lighthouse was once a handsome wood frame structure that, despite its lonely location in the bay, looked as cozy and as inviting as any home could ever be. Sadly, all that remains of that lighthouse is a few old photographs, and the derelict granite pier upon which it once proudly stood."

Withstanding Storms

First constructed in 1875 to help protect mariners from the far-reaching presence of the deadly Cross Ledge Shoal, the lighthouse by the same name served only 35 years before being decommissioned in 1910. At the time, the United States Lighthouse Service felt the newly constructed lights nearby at Elbow of Cross Ledge and Miah Maull Shoal were more than sufficient enough to protect ships in the main channel from the underwater dangers lurking in the vicinity.

The venerable lighthouse was a tough customer during both its active days and its long goodbye brought on by abandonment. The sentinel stood strong when the great hurricane of October 1878 wreaked havoc throughout Delaware Bay. And despite incurring some damage, the light's fourth order Fresnel lens continued to faithfully send out a guiding beam to mariners throughout the duration of the tempest. Cross Ledge Lighthouse was equally up to the task in the winter of 1892-93, when "Old Man Winter" hurled a formidable combination of ice floes and gales at the sentinel. Though the ice and storms scoured crucial riprap from the base of the granite pier, the lighthouse weathered nature's threats once again.

Once the beacon was permanently extinguished in 1910, the predictable wave of vandalism was soon to follow. After suffering 30 more years of deterioration brought about by both vandals and Mother Nature, the military settled on making the lighthouse "useful" again in the early 1940s.

"The military was interested in the deserted structure, because they had designated the former lighthouse as a target for training missions involving aircraft and pilots stationed nearby," said lighthouse historian Jim Gowdy. During World War II, numerous sites were designated as targets in the Delaware Bay area for training missions involving strafing, dive bombing, glide bombing, masthead bombing and rocket firing."

During these training missions, formations of fighter planes roared across the skies, each sortie taking turns diving on the helpless Cross Ledge Lighthouse before releasing or sending its target practice payloads hurtling towards the water-locked structure. The aim of many pilots was true, while others missed—their "ordinance" falling harmlessly in the Delaware Bay.

"Contrary to popular belief, no live bombs were used," said Carole Reily, known in many circles as The Lighthouse Lady. "The planes dropped flour sack markers and wooden boxes filled with lime. This enabled the pilots to see if they hit their mark." In addition to such makeshift "ordinance," fighter planes such as the Douglas Dauntless dive-bombers utilized 7-pound cast-iron practice bombs on the lighthouse to enhance their skills.

Despite such indignant treatment, Cross Ledge Lighthouse stubbornly refused to surrender its overall exterior appearance. "A military photograph of the building, dated May 23, 1945, shows the structure to be in surprisingly good condition, considering the passage of time involved," said Gowdy. "Outwardly, everything seemed to be intact except the upper part of the cupola, which was missing."

Tough to the End

The long goodbye for Cross Ledge Lighthouse would tarry on for yet another incredible 17 years, but by 1962 it would be man—not time or Mother Nature—who would ensure the final chapter containing the beacon's demise was finally written.

Reportedly, the United States Coast Guard, for safety reasons, razed the shell of Cross Ledge Lighthouse. The fire and subsequent removal of debris erased nearly every vestige of a resilient sentinel that seemingly refused to "give up the ghost" without a long and tenacious fight.

Today, only the granite base remains. Local fishermen now refer to the site as the "abandoned light" or "flattop," and though the lighthouse no longer stands to safeguard the mariner, its massive base serves as a restful stopover for seagulls, cormorants and other birds.

Cross Ledge Lighthouse Facts and Figures

• The Cross Ledge Lighthouse was lit for the first time on December 8, 1875, though it would not be until 1877-78 when the permanent structure was fully completed.
• The *1878 Description of Light Sites for the Fourth District* describes Cross Ledge Lighthouse as a two-story building, "with mansard roof, surmounted by a cylindrical watch-room and lantern." The color scheme of the lighthouse included a white dwelling, with lead-colored trim, green shutters and a lantern room painted black.
• The light source was a Funck lamp set inside a fourth order Fresnel lens that showed a flashing white light every 15 seconds, approximately 58 feet above mean low water.
• Cross Ledge Lighthouse was decommissioned on February 1, 1910, and razed in 1962.

Photo of a modern replica of the original lighthouse by Bob Trapani, Jr.

Tucker's Beach Lighthouse
New Jersey

Bob Trapani, Jr.

Hungry Ocean
Would Not Be Denied

When the federal government established lighthouses along America's vast coastline, it was with the intention of placing the warning beacon on or closest to the danger it was being commissioned to mark. In many cases, this meant that a lighthouse was purposely placed in harm's way and, thus, its legacy would be commingled with accounts of both lives saved and prodigious battles with Mother Nature.

In the case of Tucker's Beach Lighthouse (also known as Little Egg Harbor Light), its tenure upon the barrier island would be filled with the fears and realities of erosion stemming from the beacon's stand on ever shifting sands.

A clear picture of the environment upon which Tucker's Beach Light once resided is eloquently described within the article entitled, "The Riders of the Light" by Jill Richmond and Carla Coutts-Miners. According to the authors of the feature, "The island was never posh, but rather primitive, windswept and ultimately subject to the ravaging ocean and bay tides. Added to the list of nature's elements of destruction were the merciless storms that inevitably pound a barrier island like Tucker's."

More Than One Structure

The first lighthouse established on Tucker's Island in 1848 was not a friend to all mariners. In fact, some seafaring captains downright despised the light for showing what they considered an inferior light that actually proved to be more of a hazard than an aid to navigation.

Strangely enough, the Tucker's Beach Lighthouse, or Little Egg Harbor Beacon, would remain active for only 11 short years until 1859. The reasons for discontinuing the light remain shrouded, but historians Richmond and Coutts-Miners offer a couple of plausible explanations, saying, "The most likely answer lies in the continuous shifting sands the island was subject to; coupled with the inlet opening and closing, thus rendering the beacon more confusing than reassuring. Adding to the possible demise of the original Tucker's Beach Light was the addition of the Absecon Lighthouse to the south."

Apparently the local watermen, and possibly even a few sea captains, must not have approved of the decision to discontinue the lighthouse on Tucker's Island because seven years later Congress appropriated $5,000 for repairing and relighting the abandoned beacon. On June 20, 1867, a bright beam of light emitting from a 4th order Fresnel lens showed forth again from the sands of the fragile barrier island.

In order for mariners to distinguish the Tucker's Beach from other coastal lighthouses, the characteristics of a fixed white light, varied by six consecutive red flashes at intervals of 10 seconds was deployed. By 1879 the United States Lighthouse Service built a new keeper's quarters and decided to construct a new light tower that would

Photo courtesy of Tuckerton Seaport Collection

Tucker's Beach Lighthouse is shown falling into the surf on October 12, 1927.

surmount the building. The old lighthouse was then converted into a storage shed for oil.

Though the insatiable appetite of the Atlantic Ocean would ceaselessly gnaw at Tucker's Island, the next 48 years at the light station were nothing out of the ordinary. But the tranquility that became a way of life on the barrier beach was about to be altered forever as 1919 gave way to a new decade. "By 1920, the irreversible damage being inflicted upon the sands of Tucker's Island was beginning to take its toll," said historians Richmond and Coutts-Miners.

Victim of Storms and Tides

Powerful storms during the five-year period between 1920 and 1925 severely consumed much of the island and the buildings that once graced its shoreline. Cottages and hotels literally swallowed by the encroaching seas.

With the outset of 1927 it became painfully obvious that Tucker's Beach Lighthouse was doomed to soon succumb to an angry King Neptune. The island itself continued to disappear at an alarming rate, leaving very little protection sand-wise in front and around the threatened beacon. The icy seas from a damaging winter tempest in February 1927 reached the front doorstep of the lighthouse, and during the height of the mayhem, succeeded in carrying away the foundation out from under the porch.

The storm's damaging overtures frightened keeper Arthur Rider, who hastily conveyed to the United States Lighthouse Service that unless the sentinel was moved immediately, it would most certainly be lost. To back up his anxiety-filled observations, keeper Rider went on to say, "I might add that the old hotel that stood about 200 feet away and another house about 500 feet away, was washed down and totally destroyed."

Keeper Rider's aim was to have someone from the Lighthouse Service inspect the ill-fated station, so that his recommendations might be acted upon. As is the case with many concerns that require governmental intervention, the pressing issues at Tucker's Beach Lighthouse did not immediately take precedence over other matters at hand.

Six more months passed, and still no inspectors made the trek to the barrier island to assess the light's dire situation. This precarious dilemma that was about to grow much worse, and on August 26, 1927, another storm swept over the vulnerable location. This time the damaged incurred from the wind and sea snapped the remaining patience of Keeper Rider.

Abandoning the Structure

The frayed nerves of the keeper inspired him to ask permission to vacate the light station. In his daily log keeper Rider penned, "The front porch is resting on only one broken pier and it pulled away from the posts, leaving the roof and posts hanging in air 7 feet above the ground." On August 28th Rider documented that the "front porch of this station was washed down and carried away by the sea yesterday afternoon."

An inspection was made following the storm but to Keeper Rider's dismay, he was asked to remain on duty despite the fact that Tucker's Beach Lighthouse was all but uninhabitable. One long and harrowing month would pass before the United States Lighthouse Service informed Keeper Arthur Rider that the doomed beacon was to be decommissioned on September 30, 1927.

Once the light was extinguished for the final time on the morning of the 30th of September, Keeper Rider retired—no doubt relieved that he had survived his terrifying ordeal of keeping the light burning bright while the seas taunted him with each storm and overreaching high tide in 1927.

Yet despite his "freedom," Keeper Rider didn't venture far from the lighthouse. In fact, he took the occasion to inform the United States Lighthouse Service of the details involving the ultimate demise of his old friend. Excerpted comments from each letter stated:

> October 10, 1927: "Tucker Beach Lighthouse is so much undermined that it has started to sag and lean toward the ocean."
>
> October 13, 1927: "Tower and dwelling except dining room and kitchen upset in the surf yesterday and was broken up and washed away by the sea."
>
> October 14, 1927: "The dining room and kitchen of the Tucker Beach Lighthouse, which was badly wrecked when the main part of the building pulled from it and upset in the surf, was completely destroyed by fire yesterday afternoon."

Ravaging seas also claimed the abandoned U.S. Life-Saving Station that stood on the island, with the lone remaining struc-ture—the old schoolhouse—consumed by the tides in 1938 dur-ing a great northeast storm. Tucker's Island itself finally disap-peared altogether from the seascape in 1952, when the fragile strip of landscape lost its long and arduous battle with the relentless power of the Atlantic Ocean.

Tucker's Beach Lighthouse Facts and Figures

• The first lighthouse on Tucker's Island—often referred to as the Little Egg Harbor Beacon—was constructed in 1848 and stood 40 feet above the water. The original light source was comprised of 15 lamps and reflectors that shined a fixed white light to sea. By 1854, the United States Lighthouse Service refit-ted the inferior beacon with a fourth order Fresnel lens.

• The first lighthouse was discontinued in 1859, but by 1866, Congress appropriated $5,000 to reestablish the light as an aid to navigation.

• During 1879, the United States Lighthouse Service built a new Tucker's Beach Lighthouse adjacent to the old beacon. The new lighthouse stood 46 above the sea and was equipped with a fourth order Fresnel lens.

• The lighthouse was discontinued on September 30, 1927, and was destroyed by the power of the sea on October 12, 1927.

• The Tuckerton Seaport has constructed a wonderful replica of the Tucker's Beach Lighthouse at the seaport. One of the many displays inside the lighthouse is the gorgeous third order Fresnel lens that once served at Brandywine Shoal Lighthouse in Delaware Bay.

To learn more about the Tuckerton Seaport, visit the web site: www.tuckertonseaport.org

Tuckerton Seaport
120 West Main Street, P.O. Box 52
Tuckerton, New Jersey 08087
Phone: 609-296-8868

Photo by Bob Trapani, Jr.

Delaware Breakwater East End Lighthouse
Delaware

Bob Trapani, Jr.

Endless Din
of Horn and Storm

Some lighthouses might have been considered idyllic settings where golden sands and ocean blue met to form a seaside paradise, but Delaware Breakwater East End Lighthouse was not one of them.

Lighthouse historian Jim Gowdy keenly observed this fact, stating, "Visiting the lighthouse on a warm and sunny day is quite different than living at the lighthouse day in and day out as a keeper, through days of chilling winds and wave tossed seas." Gowdy went on to say, "It must have been a difficult life at the Delaware Breakwater East End Lighthouse, with land in full view, but not being able to go there except on leave."

Winter's icy winds and the detachment from land at Cape Henlopen were not the only issues for the keepers of the light to contend with though. For being stationed at the 1885 Delaware Breakwater East End Lighthouse meant that men were to be subjected to what must have seemed like an endless din of storm and horn.

When awesome seas, harrowing winds and torrents of rain weren't pounding the exposed 56-foot structure during fierce tempests, the inescapable and unnerving roar of the light station's fog signal reverberated through every square inch of the sentinel. In fact, the second class Daboll trumpet at Delaware Breakwater East End Light sounded so much due to thick weather in the late 1800s that the lighthouse garnered the distinction of being Delaware Bay's "noisiest" beacon.

Though the fog signal was a critical component to safeguarding mariners from the deadly effects of fog and thick weather, life inside the lighthouse was hardly conducive to a peaceful existence during such occasions for its keepers. A 1984 U.S. Coast Guard engineering report stated that the Delaware Breakwater East End Lighthouse, "measures 22 feet in outside diameter at the base tapering to 18 feet at just below the watch level." Being confined to a cylinder with such restrictive living space—especially during long and frigid winters, must have been both a mental and physical hardship for many a keeper.

Sounds Through the Fog

Hearing the bellowing sound of the fog signal—sometimes for days on end—was just the beginning of the keeper's trials. While being forced to endure the deafening sound, the men also had to "feed" the fog signal machinery. During the station's first few years of service, the fog signal sounded up to 900 hours a year and consumed over 12,000 pounds of coal. Could you imagine being a keeper—forced to not only listen to this terrifying sound machine, but also to shovel thousands of pounds of coal into it to keep it going?

Life aboard Delaware Breakwater East End Lighthouse during these periods was anything but fun, yet the men not only endured but also learned to adapt. Before long, the men could anticipate the exact moment the horn's characteristics were going to sound, and thereby would halt their conversations in midstream each time until the blast faded. In fact, the keepers learned to sleep with the horn as well—actually waking up when it stopped or broke down.

The worst time of audible chaos inside Delaware Breakwater East End Lighthouse was when the fog signal was screaming out its warning over the horrifying din of a raging maelstrom. During these tense moments, it's hard to imagine the lightkeepers getting any meaningful rest. No doubt the action of violent storm seas shuddering the tower and thoughts of whether the lighthouse could withstand such pounding proved quite disconcerting. Adding to this dilemma was the natural concern for the safety of ships that routinely sought refuge behind the massive stone wall upon which the lighthouse stood.

The Delaware Breakwater, built over a period of 40 years—from 1829 to 1869—is constructed of heavy stones, many weighing up to six tons, to form a wall of protection for ships during northeast gales. Between Sandy Hook, New Jersey, and Cape Charles, Virginia, Delaware Breakwater is the only safe harbor along the Atlantic seaboard, and thus was world renowned to sailing vessels of all international flags.

Though the breakwater was designed to save lives, which it accomplished time and again, the jagged stonewall could also snuff out the breath of life without a moment's notice. Wooden sailing ships and their crews caught behind the Delaware Breakwater during a strong northwest wind could suddenly find themselves in a desperate struggle for survival against the terrorizing winds.

Wreck of the 'Mary Rogers'

One such occasion occurred on January 20, 1892, when the unsuspecting crew of the *Mary Rogers* was thrown against "the stone pile" by the force of wind and sea on a night of stormy horror where the line of life and death proved to be a tightrope of fateful choices.

The *1892 Annual Report of the United States Life-Saving Service* sets the scene on this deadly night, stating, "The British schooner *Mary Rogers*, of Arichat, Nova Scotia, left Port Spain, Trinidad, December 24, 1891, bound to Philadelphia, Pennsylvania, with asphalt. After a tempestuous voyage the vessel arrived about midnight of January 19, 1892, off the entrance to the Delaware River, during a heavy northeast gale, with rain and sleet, which increased in force as the night advanced, accompanied with snow."

By the time the *Mary Rogers* reached the Delaware Breakwater the vessel's decks, rigging and sails were encased in ice. The United States Life-Saving Service annual report entry on the wreck stated that the master, Captain William Rogers, was unfamiliar with the anchorage area and "seeing a vessel near at hand riding out the gale, decided to anchor the schooner."

The captain then ordered his crew—now exhausted and frozen to the bone, to drop both of the ship's anchors and to take down the ice-covered sails. The crew managed to accomplish this strenuous task in the face of the snowstorm, being encouraged that their location behind the wall and near the guiding beam of Delaware Breakwater East End Lighthouse would protect them from the turbulent Atlantic Ocean.

Unbeknownst to the captain and crew, they could not have picked a more dangerous place to hunker down in the storm. In the meantime, the lifesaving service annual report goes on to say, "With feelings of security all hands gathered in the cabin for necessary warmth. On the flood tide the vessel lay uneasily, and at a quarter before 6 o'clock the smaller cable parted, while the larger anchor, probably being afoul, failed to hold, and the schooner began dragging, finally fetching up on the outside of the Delaware Breakwater about one hundred yards from the beacon, at the east end, where she at once began leaking."

Throughout this horrific experience, Delaware Breakwater East End Lighthouse continued to send out a bright light and sound its bellowing fog signal through the elements, but the warnings were useless to the *Mary Rogers*, which was smashed against the razor-sharp breakwater wall against its will.

The crew was petrified at the sudden turn of events and worked feverishly according to the report, which stated, "At the time of striking, the yawl was upon the main hatch. To cut the lashings and launch her over the side was the work of only a few moments, and with the painter fast on board the schooner the stern of the boat just touched the stones of the breakwater."

The tremendous seas pounding away at the shattered ship gave warning to the sailors aboard that time was short. Willing to risk the uncertainty of crossing from the precarious stern of the ship onto the slippery breakwater, the captain and three crewmen wasted little time scrambling to safety. Knowing the escape route from the ill-fated vessel was just about ready to give way, the four men shouted urgent pleas to the sailing master and the ship's cook to follow suit as quickly as possible.

For reasons unexplained, the two men aboard the ship decided to gather their personal effects despite the fact that the cabin of the ship was being inundated by icy sea water. Moments later the shattering sound of wood revealed that the stern of the yawl–which was the lone means of escape, was swept away. The sailors on the breakwater shouted out once more in an effort to bring the two men topside and alert them of the dire turn of events.

The lifesaving service report then stated, "Urging the sailing master to follow, the cook sprang into the boat, striking the bottom with such force that his feet went through the frail planking, but he scrambled out with the aid of his comrades just as a sea dashed the boat against the rocks, grinding it in pieces."

Though the cook barely cheated the hands of death, the experience proved too much for the sailing master, William Landrey, who was now paralyzed with fright. The crewmen on the breakwater repeatedly begged and pleaded with Mr. Landrey to jump into the storm-tossed waters—this being his only hope to escape doom, but the man refused. In the next moment, the splintered schooner fell on its side and slipped further off the stone wall. At this point, the seas began to completely wash over the battered derelict.

The detailed entry in the lifesaving report goes on to say, "Evidently, stupefied by his appalling situation, Landrey clung to the rigging, making no effort to save himself, while those already on the stones, their numbers increased by the arrival of the two light-keepers, were powerless to aid him."

The storm seas washed the sailing master from the rigging as his horrified crewmates watched helplessly. According to the report, "In the darkness he was finally lost to view, but in a few moments reappeared on the crest of a wave, which threw him violently on the stones and left him in a cavity, from which the people on the breakwater succeeded by joining hands in rescuing him with difficulty."

Photo by Ann-Marie Trapani

The Delaware Breakwater East End Lighthouse, off the coast at Lewes

Once Mr. Landrey was pulled to safety, the lighthouse keepers led the men along the top of the treacherous stone wall and into the warm confines of Delaware Breakwater East End Lighthouse. In the meantime, one of the men undertook the hazardous duty of walking westward along the ice-covered breakwater at 7 o'clock in the morning—about a half-mile's distance in the midst of the raging snowstorm. The purpose of his trek was to alert the telegraph office that stood on the other end of the stone wall of the shipwreck and the urgent need for a doctor to come to the lighthouse.

The light inside the structure revealed the gruesome extent of the sailing master's condition. Mr. Landrey was suffering from terrible bruises and multiple lacerations to his body, which he incurred after being dashed against the massive stone wall. Barely conscious, the men also realized that the sailing master severely dislocated his shoulder. Though every effort was made to make Mr. Landrey comfortable, the men were unable to render medical aid until the arrival of a doctor.

The United States Life-Saving Service crew at Lewes received the message from the telegraph office of the shipwreck and made their way to Delaware Breakwater East End Lighthouse around 9 a.m. in the station's surfboat. Unfortunately, the doctor was to be delayed another hour, arriving after 10 a.m. on a tugboat. When Doctor Orr entered the lighthouse he immediately started to administer medical aid to Mr. Landrey.

The lifesaving service report described the situation, saying, "In spite of Dr. Orr's efforts to resuscitate the wounded man, he sank rapidly, and soon died from exhaustion and the results of his injuries. The captain of the schooner testified that the sailing master was old and feeble and had been in poor health during the entire voyage."

The lifesavers eventually escorted the survivors of the wreck, with the doctor and the body of the dead man, back to the Lewes Station. Mr. Landrey was later interred on the grounds of the nearby Marine Hospital.

Bob Trapani, Jr.

Delaware Breakwater East End Lighthouse
Facts and Figures

- The Delaware Breakwater was completed in 1885 and lit for the first time on October 2, 1885.
- A second class Daboll trumpet was installed at the light station in November 1885 to serve as a fog signal.
- The lighthouse is 56 feet tall and once showed a light from a fourth order Fresnel lens, 60.5 feet above mean high water to sea. The light could be seen to 13 nautical miles.
- Delaware Breakwater East End Lighthouse was automated on July 11, 1950, and decommissioned as an active aid to navigation in 1996.
- The state of Delaware assumed ownership of the Delaware Breakwater East End Lighthouse from the Federal government on February 5, 1999.
- The Delaware River & Bay Authority signed a historic lease on the lighthouse with the state of Delaware on November 12, 2001.
- The Delaware River & Bay Lighthouse Foundation (www.delawarebaylights.org) and the Delaware River & Bay Authority (www.drba.net and www.capemaylewesferry.com) signed an operating agreement on August 10, 2004, for the preservation and educational utilization of Delaware Breakwater East End Lighthouse.
- The Delaware Breakwater East End Lighthouse is planned to be open to the general public to enjoy historic tours inside the beacon for the first time in June 2005.

Photo courtesy of U.S. Coast Guard

Delaware Breakwater West End Lighthouse
Delaware

House of Misery

Lightkeepers on the Delaware Bay had to be prepared to endure a multitude of hardships, that included isolation, storms and insects just to name a few. The one comfort for the men was being able to take refuge inside a stout lighthouse when Mother Nature went awry on the outside. On nights when storm-tossed waters buffeted their lighthouse mercilessly, the keepers of the lights would hunker down in their warm and safe confines—all except the men who served at Delaware Breakwater West End Lighthouse.

For lightkeepers assigned to this deplorably constructed beacon, their "refuge" might have been more aptly referred to as a house of misery.

The light station was built in 1849 to mark the western end of the Delaware Breakwater. Lighthouse records show that Thomas J. Truxton was appointed the first keeper, though it's probably not a reach to say Mr. Truxton was less than happy with the condition of the newly constructed building. A scathing inspection of the lighthouse two years later profoundly bears out the fact of the light station's awful construction.

Unflattering Report

The June 25, 1851, congressional report began by stating, "Floor of southern pine plank covered with sheet copper; leaks so badly that it is almost impossible to occupy the apartments below; it always leaked . . . six, 14-inch spherical reflectors; miserable things and badly used; scratched and bruised; new when put up."

The report continued to spew negative comments about the lighthouse, saying, "Dome of lantern caulked with canvas to keep out the wind and the rain, (stuck around lower part of dome); no curtains; lamps are bad . . . lantern never good; copper broken adrift above the gallery; dome black with soot; sashes black; no paint; dirty; no ventilation; no proper place to keep the oil, etc.; oil kept in the old lighthouse. Tanks are placed in the arches, which were built to allow the sea to pass through it under the house—apparently to pass the tide wave; but the tanks are placed so far below the level of the crown of the arch, it must necessarily intercept it, and endanger the whole building. The tanks are very deficient in support."

Even the light source itself did not escape the wrath of the inspection report. Apparently, the temporary light that was still standing in 1851 was actually better positioned to show a good light than the new lighthouse—quite an embarrassing situation for the federal government.

According to the report, "It is impossible to see the red portion of this light, if at all, at a greater distance than a mile to a mile and a half. The light is not located on the spot which it ought to occupy, because the breakwater is not yet completed to that point, and it is believed that the old light, which is yet standing, would have served the purposes of navigation as well as the new one."

Closing the "gap" in the breakwater rendered the Delaware Breakwater West End Lighthouse obsolete in 1903.

One can imagine what a miserable existence it must have been at Delaware Breakwater West End Lighthouse. The structure was unable to prevent wind and rain from entering the building and thus, the lighthouse must have been ceaselessly damp and cold, especially in wintertime. When the icy winds swept over Delaware Bay at the height of "Old Man Winter's" annual reign, Keeper Truxton and others were not able to seek the warmth and comfort generally associated with better-constructed lighthouses.

In fact, rainwater and moisture penetrating the structure must have periodically ruined the keeper's furniture and personal belongings. Even walking across the wood floors must have been a frustrating experience, as water would accumulate on the surface during stormy weather. Keeper Truxton was compensated $50 a year more than his fellow comrades—possibly for having to endure the wretched living conditions at Delaware Breakwater West End Lighthouse. But extra money was hardly a comfort when winter nights proved long, cold and wet.

Keeping Up Appearances

As bad as conditions were at Delaware Breakwater West End Lighthouse, the keepers tried their best to avoid letting the public see this uncomplimentary side of lighthouse life. Light stations, in general, were a source of pride to both the federal government and the community in which they served. Therefore, every effort was made to ensure that the public face of the lighthouse was revealed in a positive manner. Evidently, the keepers became quite proficient at making Delaware Breakwater West End Light appear "homey"—certainly not an easy task by any stretch of the imagination.

The *Peninsular News & Advertiser* from Milford, Delaware, on February 8, 1862, gave great testimony to this fact, stating, "Everything about the premises is in the nicest condition, under the care of the keeper, Mr. John Burton and his assistant to whose gentlemanly kindness we are indebted for much entertaining and useful information received during the hour we spent about the buildings."

The reporter's account of his experience at the lighthouse must have occurred on a warmer day—even for February, for his opinion might have been different had the harrowing winds and

111

icy rain of a winter northeaster been penetrating the lighthouse and dousing the interior drip by drip.

A damp environment that chilled the keepers to the bone on the interior of the lighthouse was not the only concern, as the exterior of the lighthouse was no better.

In what was surely a frustrating report to convey, the *1878 Annual Report of the Lighthouse Board* was forced to tell Congress that, "For sometime past the breakwater has been settling, causing cracks in the walls of the lighthouse. The pier under the northwest corner of the lighthouse has been removed, the upper stones of the breakwater taken away, and a new pier has been built, starting 12 feet below the original foundation. Thus, it is hoped, will prevent it from settling farther."

This dilemma must have created great anxiety for the light-keepers—especially when storm seas lashed at the beacon during severe weather. Nearly all keepers of water-locked lighthouses pondered from time to time about whether or not their house of refuge would hold up during the fury of a great tempest, but given the deplorable conditions at Delaware Breakwater West End Lighthouse, this concern must have taken on a more serious meaning.

Things were to grow worse the following year as the horrific hurricane of October 1878 wreaked havoc on the light station, causing significant harm to the property. Due to the storm's widespread damage to many lighthouses in Delaware Bay, repairs at Delaware Breakwater West End Lighthouse were carried out over a period of two years.

The *1879 Annual Report of the Light-House Board* stated that "Some repairs were now in progress," but it would be another year before the keepers of this lighthouse were provided with a more "shored-up" structure. The 1880 report records the additional repairs, stating, "A new boat landing was constructed, and the gallery around the structure repaired, new window-shutters were placed on the dwelling, and a new pump was placed in the water cistern. The structure was painted, inside and out. The fog-bell frame was strengthened, the new bell and striking apparatus were put up, and the machinery was protected by a small house."

The constant upkeep to the lighthouse was predictably ongoing despite the extensive repairs. By 1881, steps leading from the landing area were rebuilt thanks to the scouring effects of ice floes that carried the previous set away on the tides. Seven years later the great storm of March 1888 hammered the lighthouse and inflicted some minor damage, but it was the hurricane of September 1889 that delivered more of a destructive blow to the light station.

According to the 1890 annual report, Delaware Breakwater West End Lighthouse witnessed its fog bell and frame tower carried away by tremendous seas, as was the station's outbuildings, plank walks and landing steps. Though the repairs were enacted and divers did recover the bell in the water below, the fog signal was never reestablished at the lighthouse.

The one act more than any that spelled the doom of this forsaken light station was when the Federal government decided to fill in the "gapway" between Delaware Breakwater and the nearby icebreaker. Once the area was connected and filled in by a wall of stone, the value of the lighthouse as an aid to navigation was greatly diminished, other than serving as the front range light for the Delaware Breakwater Range from 1881 to 1903. But changes in the cape region made the range obsolete by 1903, and the Delaware Breakwater West End Lighthouse was decommissioned.

The Maritime Exchange, which occupied a small reporting station adjacent to the lighthouse on the stone wall, was granted permission to use the building for its activities. The Exchange occupied the old lighthouse until 1942, when it moved their operation permanently on land at Cape Henlopen. The lighthouse then reverted back to the Federal government, but with no further use for such a dilapidated building, time, the elements and vandalism began to sound the sentinel's death-knell.

Finally, in 1959, the United States Coast Guard razed the structure for safety reasons, leaving only ghostly piles of bricks on the breakwater as proof of where it once stood watch during the golden age of Lewes Harbor.

Delaware Breakwater West End Lighthouse
Facts and Figures

• Records indicate that a temporary light was maintained on the west end of the Delaware Breakwater as early as 1838, though the lighthouse itself wasn't completed until October 1849.

• The *1858 List of Lighthouses, Lighted Beacons and Floating Lights in the United States* lists Delaware Breakwater West End Lighthouse as being outfitted with a fourth order Fresnel lens that displayed a light 47 feet above sea level. The light could be seen up to ten nautical miles.

• The station's importance on the Delaware Breakwater warranted a fog bell struck by machinery to be installed at the light station to help warn ships of the dangers associated with the breakwater being obscured during periods of fog or thick weather.

• The *1878 List of Towers, Beacons, Buoys, Stakes and other Day-Marks* in the Fourth Lighthouse District lists the lighthouse as being a whitewashed brick structure with a black lantern.

• The Delaware Breakwater West End Lighthouse served as the front light for the Delaware Breakwater Range from 1881 to 1903 before being decommissioned that same year.

Selected Bibliography

Bachand, Robert G.—*Northeast Lights: Lighthouses and Lightships, Rhode Island to Cape May, New Jersey,* Sea Sports Pub., Norwalk, Conn., 1989

Bailey, Robert—*Sentinel of the Jersey Cape: The Story of the Cape May Lighthouse,* Cape Publishing, Inc., Cape May, New Jersey, 2001

Beach, John W.—*Cape Henlopen Lighthouse,* Henlopen Publishing Company, Dover, Delaware, 1970

Blunt's American Coast Pilot, 1850

Coshocton Daily Age, September 17, 1903

Daily Republican, Illinois, April 25, 1899

De Wire, Elinor—*Guardians of the Lights: Stories of the U.S. Lighthouse Keepers,* Pineapple Press, Inc., Sarasota, Florida, 1995

De Wire, Elinor—*The Lighthouse Almanac: A Compendium of Science, History, & Fascinating Lore about our Favorite Seamarks,* Sentinel Publications, Gales Ferry, Connecticut, 2000

Delaware River & Bay Lighthouse Foundation Web Site: http://www.delawarebaylights.org

Elyria Reporter, Ohio, July 7, 1905

Grand Rapids Tribune, Wisconsin, December 6, 1905

Gowdy, Jim and Kim Ruth—*Guiding Lights of the Delaware River & Bay,* Jim Gowdy, Sweetwater, New Jersey, 1999

Hereford Inlet Lighthouse Web Site: http://www.herefordlighthouse.org/main.htm

Johnson, Arnold Burges—*The Modern Lighthouse Service,* 1890

Jones, Stephen—*Harbor of Refuge*, University Press of New England, Hanover, New Hampshire, 2000

Lewes Historical Society—"Some of the Experiences of John W. (Jack) Hill in the Lighthouse Service from 1917 to 1941" (unpublished)

Lighthouse Digest Web Site: http://www.lhdigest.com

Lima News, Ohio, June 24, 1930

Lima Times Democrat, Ohio, March 7, 1913

Lincoln Daily News, Nebraska, March 12, 1914

List of Lighthouses, Lighted Beacons and Floating Lights in the United States, 1858

List of Towers, Beacons, Buoys, Stakes and other Day-Marks in the Fourth Lighthouse, 1878

Lynch-Morris, Dorothy—"Burning Schooner" (unpublished)

Mid-Atlantic Center for the Arts Web Site: http://www.capemaymac.org

Murray, Steve—*A Guide to the Hereford Inlet Lighthouse Gardens*, Hereford Inlet Lighthouse Commission, North Wildwood, NJ, 2001

New Jersey Lighthouse Society Web Site: http://www.njlhs.burlco.org

New Oxford Item, Pennsylvania, September 13, 1895

New York Times, New York City, March 21, 1926

Peninsular News & Advertiser, Milford, Delaware, February 8, 1862

Philadelphia Evening Bulletin, Pennsylvania, May 2, 1938; Dec. 19, 1954

Ramsey, Kelvin and Marijke J. Reilly—"The Hurricane of October 21-24, 1878," *Delaware Geological Survey, Special Publication No. 22*, Office of Publications, University of Delaware, 2002

Reily, Carole—"Cross Ledge Lighthouse," *The Bay Run*, Autumn, 2000

Richmond, Jill and Carla Coutts-Miners—"The Riders of the Light" (unpublished)

Spencer, Harry—"Japanese Beetles Galore" (unpublished)

Taylor, Robert C.—Excerpts from Personal Journal, courtesy of Sherry Mitchell (unpublished)

Trapani, Jr., Bob—"Irresistible Force Meets Immovable Object," *Lighthouse Digest*, July, 2002

Trapani, Jr., Bob—"Sudden Impact," *Lighthouse Digest*, April, 2003

Trapani, Jr., Bob—"Night Lifesavers Rescue a Lightkeeper and his Family from the Perils of the Sea," *Lighthouse Digest*, August, 2004

Trapani, Jr., Bob—"Delaware Breakwater East End Light to Welcome Visitors in 2005," *Twin Capes Traveller*, Fall, 2004

Trenton Evening Times, New Jersey, June 19, 1911

United States Coast Guard Historian's Web Site: http://www.uscg.mil/hq/g-cp/history/collect.html

United States Coast Pilot/1908—"Atlantic Coast, Part V, New York to Chesapeake Bay Entrance," U.S. Government Printing Office, Washington, D.C., 1908

United States Coast Pilot/1937—"Atlantic Coast, Section C, Sandy Hook to Cape Henry, including Delaware and Chesapeake Bays," Fourth Edition. U.S. Government Printing Office, Washington, D.C., 1937

United States Lighthouse Board Inspection Report, June 25, 1851

United States Life-Saving Service Annual Reports—1885,1892, 1904

United States Lighthouse Service Annual Reports—1872, 1875, 1878, 1879, 1880, 1884, 1885, 1890, 1897

Washington Post, Washington, D.C., May 27, 1908, and May 10, 1911

About the Author

Photo by Ann-Marie Trapani

Bob Trapani, Jr., was born in Pottstown, Pennsylvania, and now resides in Lewes, Delaware, with his wife, Ann-Marie, and their three children—Nina, Katrina and Dominic.

Bob co-founded the non-profit Delaware River & Bay Lighthouse Foundation in 1999 for the purpose of saving the State of Delaware's remaining lighthouse heritage. He serves as president of the organization and currently works full-time as a lighthouse preservationist. The Delaware River & Bay Lighthouse Foundation presently serves as the caretakers of three historic lighthouses—Harbor of Refuge, Liston Range Rear Light and Delaware Breakwater East End.

In addition to his passion for lighthouse preservation, Bob served four years—from 2000-2003—as the executive director of the 1876 Indian River Life-Saving Station Museum. During his tenure at the life-saving station, Bob authored his first book—*Journey Along the Sands: A History of Indian River Life-Saving Station*, in 2002. He also enjoys volunteering his time to the United States Coast Guard as an Auxiliarist for USCG Aids to Navigation Team, Cape May, New Jersey. Bob was awarded the prestigious U.S. Coast Guard Auxiliary Meritorious Service Award for his contributions to the field of aids to navigation from 2001 through 2003.

Bob also enjoys maritime writing and is a contributing writer for *Lighthouse Digest* magazine, Wells, Maine. In addition, his features have also appeared in other publications such as *Twin Capes Traveller* and *Wreck & Rescue* magazines. Bob also has penned a new book entitled, *Guardians of the Coast, A History of Delaware's Lighthouses*, which is due to be released in the latter part of 2005.

He also enjoys supporting other lighthouse organizations and is a proud member of the American Lighthouse Foundation, Chesapeake Chapter of the United States Lighthouse Society and the DeTour Reef Light Preservation Society, to name a few.

COMING NEXT

Lighthouses
of Maryland and Virginia

From Havre de Grace to Assateague Island . . .

Concord Point

Assateague

from Point Lookout and up the Chesapeake Bay,

Sharps Island

Thomas Point

look for more fascinating stories from Lighthouse Historian Bob Trapani, Jr.

119

More titles from Myst and Lace Publishers, Inc.

Ghost Stories

Regional History

Mystery Novels

For more information about these books,
which are available at some local and chain bookstores,
visit the web site:www.mystandlace.com, send an e-mail to
Ed Okonowicz at edo@mystandlace.com or call (410) 398-5013.
The books also are available through www.Amazon.com

. . . and you thought sharks were the only danger at the beach!

In *Terrifying Tales of the Beaches and Bays* and the sequel, award-winning author and storyteller Ed Okonowicz shares eerie accounts of spirits roaming the shore.

Read about:

- A river pilot's memorable New Year's Eve cruise

- Desperate Confederates escaping from an island prison

- Serious seekers of pirate gold

- Fishermen stranded in the icy Chesapeake Bay

- Lighthouse keepers still tending a long-gone beacon

- A most unusual "catch of the day"

- Ocean City's "Trash Rat"

- and more . . . .   **$9.95 each**

128 pages
5 1/2" x 8 1/2"
softcover
ISBN 1-890690-06-6

> Delmarva
> **beach-reading
> best sellers**

128 pages
5 1/2" x 8 1/2"
softcover
ISBN 1-890690-10-4

Treasure Hunting
by Eddie Okonowicz

Dig up your own hidden treasures with this excellent "how to" book

This book is loaded with tips on using a metal detector to hunt for relics and treasure, plus photos of numerous historical finds.

48 pages
5 1/2" x 8 1/2"
softcover
ISBN 1-890690-07-4
$6.95

To order our books

Name _____

Address _____

City_____State_____Zip Code_____

Phone _(_____)_____e-mail:_____

To receive the free *Spirits Speaks* newsletter and information on future volumes, public tours and events, send us your e-mail address, visit our web site at www.mystandlace.com or fill out the above form and mail it to us.

I would like to order the following books:

Quantity	Title	Price	Total
_____	**Lighthouses of New Jersey and Delaware**	**$11.95**	_____
_____	Baltimore Ghosts	$11.95	_____
_____	Baltimore Ghosts Teacher's Guide	$ 8.95	_____
_____	Terrifying Tales of the Beaches and Bays	$ 9.95	_____
_____	Terrifying Tales 2 of the Beaches and Bays	$ 9.95	_____
_____	Treasure Hunting	$ 6.95	_____
_____	Pulling Back the Curtain, Vol I	$ 8.95	_____
_____	Opening the Door, Vol II (second edition)	$ 9.95	_____
_____	Welcome Inn, Vol III	$ 8.95	_____
_____	In the Vestibule, Vol IV	$ 9.95	_____
_____	Presence in the Parlor, Vol V	$ 9.95	_____
_____	Crying in the Kitchen, Vol VI	$ 9.95	_____
_____	Up the Back Stairway, Vol VII	$ 9.95	_____
_____	Horror in the Hallway, Vol VIII	$ 9.95	_____
_____	Phantom in the Bedchamber, Vol IX	$ 9.95	_____
_____	Possessed Possessions	$ 9.95	_____
_____	Possessed Possessions 2	$ 9.95	_____
_____	Ghosts	$ 9.95	_____
_____	Fired! A DelMarVa Murder Mystery (DMM)	$ 9.95	_____
_____	Halloween House (DMM#2)	$ 9.95	_____
_____	Disappearing Delmarva	$38.00	_____
_____	Friends, Neighbors & Folks Down the Road	$30.00	_____
_____	Stairway over the Brandywine, A Love Story	$ 5.00	_____

*Md residents add 5% sales tax.

Please include $2.00 postage for the first book, and 50 cents for each additional book.
Make checks payable to:
    Myst and Lace Publishers

Subtotal_____
Tax*_____
Shipping_____
Total_____

Mail to: Myst and Lace Publishers, Inc.
          1386 Fair Hill Lane
          Elkton, Maryland 21921

Visit our web site at: www.mystandlace.com